access to philos

D0561696

PHILOSOPHY *of* RELIGION

Peter Cole

2nd Edition

Hodder Murray

A MEMBER OF THE HODDER HEADLINE GROUP

Some other titles in the series:

Issues of Life and Death
Michael Wilcockson   ISBN 0 340 72488 9

Introduction to the New Testament
Kevin O'Donnel   ISBN 0 340 72490 0

Religion and Science
Mel Thompson   ISBN 0 340 75771 X

Sex and Relationships
Michael Wilcockson   ISBN 0 340 72489 7

Environmental Ethics
Joe Walker   ISBN 0 340 75770 1

Theory of Knowledge
Peter Cole   ISBN 0 340 80482 3

The publisher and the Author would like to thank the following for permission to reproduce copyright photographs in this book: Figure 1, p. 18, Corbis; Figure 2, p. 37, The National Gallery; Figure 3, p. 64 and Figure 4, p. 92, AKG Photos.

Orders: please contact Bookpoint Ltd, 78 Milton Park, Abingdon, Oxon OX14 4TD. Telephone: (44) 01235 827720, Fax: (44) 01235 400454. Lines are open from 9.00–6.00, Monday to Saturday, with a 24 hour message answer service. You can also order through our website www.hoddereducation.co.uk.

British Library Cataloguing in Publication Data
A catalog

ISBN-1(
ISBN-1!

First pu
Second
Impres
Year

Copyr

All rig   d in
any fo   rding,
or any   ng
from   ited.
Futhe   d
from   don
WIT

Cove

Type
Print   er of the
Hodd

Contents

Preface

To the student

Access books are written mainly for students studying for examinations at higher level, particularly GCE Advanced Subsidiary (AS) Level and Advanced (A) Level. A number of features have been included to assist students, such as the word-lists at the beginning of chapters and the material at the end of chapters.

To use these books most effectively, you should be aware of the following features.

- The introductory chapter will set the scene for the material in the rest of the book.
- The Contents gives a break-down of the section in each chapter.
- If you turn to the relevant chapters, you will find that they are broken down further into sub-headings and bullet-points. There are sometimes also Key Issues, Key Questions, Notes and Examples to focus your attention on important points.
- The Key Words at the beginning of each chapter are for easy reference and to help you become more familiar with the technical language of the subject.
- There is also a range of typical examination questions, with some specific advice on how to answer them. Do tackle the specimen questions, planning your answers to some of them and writing some in full.

General advice on answering essay questions
Structured questions will tell you what to include. The following advice is for those questions which leave it to you to work out.

- The most important thing is to read the question carefully and work out what it really means. Make sure you understand all the words in question (you may need to check some of them in the dictionary or look up technical terms in the Word Lists in the book).
- Gather the relevant information for answering the question. You will probably *not* need everything you know on the topic. Keep to what the question is asking.
- Organise your material by drawing up a plan of paragraphs. Make sure that each paragraph is relevant to the question. Include different views within your answer (most questions require arguments for and against).
- Start with an introduction which explains in your own words what the question is asking and defines any technical words. Work through your answer in your carefully planned paragraphs. Write a brief conclusion in which you sum up your answer to the question (without repeating everything in the essay).

1 Tools for the job

KEYWORDS

philosophy – literally 'a love of wisdom'. The actual subject area is disputed and ranges from linguistic analysis to questions about ultimate reality

teleological – the study of ends or final causes, particularly as evidence for design and purpose in nature

natural theology – the use of reasoned argument to assess basic religious claims, such as the existence of God

revealed theology – claims about God derived from 'revelations' from special experiences of God or sacred writings

argument – a set of statements which is such that one of them (the conclusion) is supported or implied by the others (the premises)

proof – something that shows the truth of something

deduction – a process of reasoning by which the conclusion is shown to follow necessarily from the premises

induction – a process of reasoning that draws a general conclusion from specific instances

1 Introduction

> **KEY ISSUE** According to the philosopher A J Ayer, the business of **philosophy** is to clarify and analyse. To many students starting out on philosophy, such a view does not match their experiences. If anything, philosophy seems to make things more complex and confusing, and produce problems where none appeared before!

There may be many explanations to account for this common experience, but I think part is due to the boldness of philosophy in challenging popular common sense and basic assumptions. Philosophy is not satisfied with the claim that 'it's obvious' or 'it's common sense'. Rather, it seeks to challenge the view that common sense = truth. It can challenge beliefs that you may hold very dear, and it never claims to provide answers to the ultimate questions. Students may often end up feeling they know less than before they started!

Another difficulty experienced by students new to philosophy is the subject-specific language. Every subject study area faces this problem. However, it is important to use the right language and to do so from the start. It is essential to understand the exact meanings of technical words and to be comfortable using them. Many students try to side-step this task – a task that can be hard work – only to find themselves confused later because of some basic misunderstandings.

A philosophy book is not usually light reading or something to read just before going to sleep at bedtime! Usually it is helpful to take notes and even to write out the **arguments** for yourself, so that you are clear about the path of reasoning. Because of the often close argument, you may well find yourself having to read a page two or three times over. This is quite normal and you should not take it as a sign of failure on your part to understand.

You will find that the discipline that you develop by studying philosophy helps you in your other studies as well. It sharpens up your mind to grapple with such things as the definitions of concepts. You will become more aware of what does and does not constitute a valid argument. You will also develop the skill of following and evaluating arguments. A further benefit is that such study gives insight into the history of ideas and the debates that have accompanied them. It will force you to examine your own ideas and presuppositions. As Socrates concluded: 'Life that is not examined is life that is not worth living.'

2 Philosophy of religion

The word 'philosophy' means literally 'love of wisdom'. As I have indicated, two of the concerns of philosophy are to clarify the meanings of words and to identify ways of testing for logical coherency. It is not a subject in its own right – it is always the philosophy *of* something, such as science, education or mind. In particular, the philosophy of religion examines the general philosophical problems about religion and God. It analyses concepts such as God and eternal life, tries to determine the meaning of religious utterances and examines the nature and existence of a God or gods and the way in which God is related to the world.

Although the contents of a philosophy of religion course can vary significantly, none the less it has always been the tradition to include an examination of the classical arguments for the existence of God. There are generally considered to be five classical arguments, although there are numerous other arguments for God. Four of the five are based on observable phenomena such as the order within the universe (**teleological argument**) or the experiences of many people of things beyond the natural order (religious experience). The fifth is based on the concept of God, from which it is argued that when the concept is properly understood, it will be seen that it must have a reality in existence. We will look at these in detail in the next chapter, but before discussing the *theistic proofs* (an attempt to prove by argument that God exists) we need some 'tools of the trade'. We need to understand what constitutes a good or a bad argument.

The very idea that we can reason out the arguments for God and be convinced about them is known as **natural theology**. This assumes that we can use our cognitive faculties to reach conclusions about whether God exists or not. In this approach, no special religious authority is appealed to. This contrasts with **revealed theology** where claims about God derive from 'revelations' from special experiences of God or sacred writings. Perhaps the distinction between the two is slightly blurred since arguments can be formulated for God's existence based on, for example, religious experience or miracles. Both of these arguments claim special experiences but both still require us to reason out whether God exists.

3 Philosophical arguments

> **KEY ISSUE** The philosophy of religion has concerned itself with reasoned arguments. However, what is an argument? What constitutes a proof?

An argument can be defined as 'a set of statements which is such that one of them (the conclusion) is supported or implied by the others (the premises)', e.g.

- The Eiffel Tower is in Paris.
- Paris is in France.

Therefore the Eiffel Tower is in France.

The first two statements are the *premises*, and the third is the *conclusion*.

A *valid* argument is one where there are no mistakes in logic. Hence the above argument is a valid argument. However *beware*, not all valid arguments are therefore true, e.g.

- The Eiffel Tower is in Worthing.
- Worthing is in England.

Therefore the Eiffel Tower is in England.

There is nothing wrong with the logic here! However, there seems plenty wrong in agreeing with the conclusion. The problem is, of course that one of the premises is untrue. Hence even if the logic is impeccable, it does not mean to say that the conclusion is true. To acknowledge this problem, philosophy refers to an argument where both the logic is correct and the premises are true, as a *sound* argument.

Hence a sound argument is what we really mean by philosophical **proof**. To put it another way – a definition of proof is 'that which results from a valid argument constructed from a set of true premises'. To be compelling, the premises would have to be known to be true by those offering the proof and by those to whom it is offered. A proof is such that if you agree with the premises then you would have to agree with the conclusion. Indeed, to accept the premises and deny the conclusion would be self-contradictory.

If philosophy only considered these types of arguments then disputes between philosophers would be less numerous, and fewer philosophy books would be written. However, there is another type of argument that is less persuasive but more common, e.g.

- If it rains, I shall get wet.
- I get wet.

Therefore it rained.

I could imagine an instance where, though I agreed with the premises, I did not agree with the conclusion. For instance, I did not get wet because it rained, but because a student crept up behind me and threw a bucket of water over me! In other words, there are more ways of getting wet than just by rain. To express it more formally – the conclusion does not necessarily follow from the premises. The premises provide some, but not absolute, support for the conclusion. Indeed, to accept the premises and deny the conclusion (as we have seen) would not be self-contradictory.

As we said, philosophers are concerned with clarity, so they distinguish between the two types of argument. The first type, which we called valid is known as a *deductive* argument, whilst the second type is called *inductive*. Unfortunately this can often lead to confusion, particularly if you are an ardent fan of the detective Sherlock Holmes. Sherlock Holmes prided himself on his deductive reasoning. As far as philosophers are concerned it was **induction**! To conclude that someone has a dog because they have dog hairs on their trousers is not **deduction** but induction. After all, they could have brushed against a dog just prior to calling in at 221B Baker Street. Chapter 2 in Conan Doyle's *A Study in Scarlet* is entitled 'The science of deduction'. In this chapter Dr Watson lists the skills of Sherlock Holmes and accurately notes against his knowledge of philosophy – 'nil'!

The problem with inductive arguments is their obvious limitation of always being open to doubt and uncertainty. Equally the problem with deductive arguments is that they are also limited. It is difficult to establish the original premises, and the conclusions reached are often obvious from the original premises. Indeed, by necessity the original premises must already contain the conclusion.

All this rather theoretical introduction to arguments may seem rather irrelevant. 'When are we going to get to the philosophy?' you ask. However, identifying the key premises of a complex argument is a vital task. Setting out arguments in a formal way of premises and conclusion is also important for clarity. Assessing arguments becomes much easier and a basic check list can then be followed:

- Are the premises true?
- Is the argument valid (without logical error)?
- If inductive, how persuasive is it?

One problem is to assess 'levels of persuasiveness' of inductive arguments. Something that is convincing to one person often carries no weight with another. We need to be conscious of the various presuppositions that each of us holds, and how these affect the way we interpret the evidence. Also, we must acknowledge that different types of evidence are appropriate to the differing areas under investigation. For example, scientific evidence involves observation from which an hypothesis (a suggested explanation) is formed. This is then tested by a series of experiments. If the expected results from the experiments do not occur, a more modified hypothesis has to be formulated, taking into account the new observations. However, if the expected results *do* occur, it does *not* mean that the hypothesis is finally proven, but rather that it has escaped disproof. Obviously the more times the hypothesis escapes disproof the more certain one becomes of its truth.

In contrast, historical evidence involves assessing such things as documents, artifacts and circumstantial evidence, as well as interpreting that evidence. The conclusion reached will be on the scale of different degrees of certainty – certain, probable, possible, improbable, impossible.

Even the scientific method has become modest in its claims of proof. Scientific laws are increasingly seen as descriptions of what we expect to happen, rather than what must happen. Indeed, some would argue that nothing can be *proved* by experimental means since an infinite number of tests would be required. For instance, every time we heat iron, it expands. But what about the iron we have not heated? How can we be certain that iron will expand? To be certain we would have to heat every piece of iron, and even then we could never be sure that it would expand next time we heated it.

Answering questions on Chapter I

By the end of this chapter you should understand the difference between a deductive and an inductive argument, as well as the various connotations of the word *proof.*

Many questions will include in their phrasing the word *proof,* so it is important to be able to make comments on its different shades of meaning, especially in relationship to the topic on which the question focuses.

Deductive	Inductive
If its premises are true, then its conclusion must be true.	If its premises are true, then its conclusion could still be false.
The premises provide absolute support for the conclusion.	The premises provide some, but not absolute, support for the conclusion.
The information contained in the conclusion is completely contained in the premises.	

An argument is either deductive or inductive. If the premises provide *no* support for the conclusion then it is a non-argument.

Degree of premises' support for conclusion		
Non-arguments	**Inductive arguments**	**Deductive arguments**
None	Weak Reasonable Strong	Absolute

It is a useful exercise to read an argument and then to try to express it by means of premises and a conclusion. Try to do this with the following extract from a debate in Parliament on abortion:

> *Mr. Enoch Powell*: I beg to move, that the Bill be now read a second time. The Bill has a single and simple purpose. It is to render it unlawful for a human embryo created by in vitro [laboratory] fertilisation to be used as the subject of experiment or, indeed, in any other way or for any other purpose except to enable a woman to bear a child ...
>
> It is argued ... that to permit the use of a fertilised embryo for research would open the way to new and useful medical knowledge. I do not stand here as a layman to dispute that. True, I must admit I have a suspicion that the inquiring human spirit will, if denied one avenue of arriving at truth and information, speedily find other ways of doing so. I have also been impressed to find profound difference of opinion on this very point among people apparently equally qualified in the medical profession and in the sciences.
>
> Nevertheless, I do not ask the House to reject the proposition. On the contrary, I ask the House to face it. I ask the House, in coming to a decision, to make the assumption that by means of what the Bill will prohibit, useful and beneficial knowledge would in future be obtained. I ask the House to exercise a choice – and to decide that nevertheless the moral, human and social cost of that information being obtained in a way that outrages the instincts of so many is too great a price to pay.
>
> From 'Unborn Children (Protection) Bill', *Parliamentary Debates* (Hansard) Volume 73, No. 62, 15 February 1985

2 The nature of God

KEYWORDS

agnostic – a person who does not believe it is possible to know whether God exists

atheism – a belief that there is no God

deism – the view that God created the universe but is now not directly involved in creation

immanent – existing or remaining in. In theology it refers to God's involvement in creation

incorporeal – without material form

materialism – the view that the material universe is all that exists

middle knowledge – God knows what every creature would do in any given set of circumstances, even if those circumstances never actually occur

omnipotent – all-powerful. Philosophers disagree as to whether this includes the power to do the logically impossible

omniscient – all-knowing. Philosophers disagree as to whether this includes middle knowledge

pantheism – the idea that the whole universe is God or part of God

theism – the belief in the existence of God

transcendent – having existence outside the universe

KEY ISSUE The very concept of God raises a number of philosophical problems concerning coherency and consistency.

1 Introduction

Theism and **materialism** are two very different views of reality. Theism is the belief that reality is made up of God Himself and all that God creates. In contrast, materialism claims that only the physical world exists and so denies the existence of God. Philosophy seeks to investigate reality by means of reason and by weighing up evidence, concerned at all times that propositions are coherent and consistent. However the very concept of God, at the centre of theism, raises a number of difficulties.

2 Terminology

According to A Thiselton (*A Concise Encyclopedia of the Philosophy of Religion*, 2002), the term 'theism' emerged in the seventeenth century to denote belief in God, in contrast to both **atheism** and **deism**. Atheism is the belief that there is no God and so the world is all there is. In contrast the agnostic is someone who has suspended judgement about the existence of a God. They are unable to decide one way or the other. Just as there is a clear difference between a theist and an atheist, so there is between a theist and a deist. A deist, like the classical theist, believes in one God who created and sustains the universe, but does not believe that God is actively involved with the world. This view sees God more of an observer than a participator. The involvement of God in miracles, for example, is not acceptable to a deist.

One other term connected with the family of 'theisms' is **pantheism**, literally meaning that God is everything. It does not see God as creator and separate from the universe He made. Indeed the universe is God and so has always existed. Although pantheism may sound similar to atheism in its belief about reality, it is in the family of 'theisms' because it argues that the universe has goals that it is pursuing. The universe is purposeful and intelligent and has direction.

3 The key attributes of God

It could be argued that it makes more sense to find out whether God exists before worrying about what God is like. However, when we are discussing the existence of God, what we are doing is asking whether there is any evidence that a particular kind of being exists. Hence the examination of the attributes of such a being will help clarify our arguments about its possible existence. At this stage no assumption is being made about its existence. When we have defined the kind of being we are talking about, we then go on to enquire whether any such being exists.

It is appropriate at this point to see how some philosophers have sought to define this being. Anselm defined God as 'that than which nothing greater can be conceived' (see Chapter 3). By this he meant that God was the greatest possible being, the one who maximised all possible qualities. Nothing could be superior or even equal to God, since to be equal with God would mean that God was not the greatest. Descartes developed this approach in his argument for God and defined God as 'a supremely perfect being'. (It should be noted that this approach to God is using the Christian tradition though it is applicable to other monotheistic faiths. For a survey of other views of God, see Chapter 3 in R. Solomon's, *The Big Questions*, 1998).

Starting from such a definition of God as 'a perfect being' may seem reasonable as it incorporates the idea of an object worthy of worship. However, the problem arises as to what are the exact attributes that a perfect being would possess. Various philosophers have attempted to list the possible attributes. For instance H P Owen (*Concepts of Deity*, (1971), R. Swinburne (*The Coherence of Theism*, 1977) and R Nash (*The Concept of God*, 1983) all identify various attributes of the nature of God associated with the classical monotheistic traditions. The key ones are:

- **Creator** – God is creator of all things other than Himself. He created the universe out of nothing ('ex nihilo') and gives it purpose. God is separate from His creation.
- **Sustainer** – the created things are totally dependent on God for their existence from moment to moment. Without God, the universe would collapse into nothingness.
- **Personal** – a basic concept of a religious life is that God can enter into relationships with people. He also performs actions.
- **Transcendent** – often expressed as God's 'otherness'. God is unique and distinct from creation. He has existence outside the created world. Balanced against this is God's immanence, denoting God's presence and action within the world.
- **Self-existent** – God depends on nothing other than Himself.
- **Eternal** – this has two aspects. One has to do with duration in that God is seen as always existing by nature rather than choice. He cannot choose to cease to exist. He is everlasting. The second aspect focuses on God's timelessness.
- **Incorporeal** – God is not a material thing. God does not occupy space to the exclusion of other things. He is not body but spirit.
- **Omnipotent** – God can do everything that is logically possible. Some, like Descartes, argue that God can also do the logically impossible. Others restrict God's power further by arguing that God can only perform acts that are consistent with God's his own nature (e.g. in 2 Timothy 2:13 St. Paul claims that 'God cannot deny Himself').
- **Omniscient** – this is often regarded as a subset of omnipotence. God knows all things and never believes anything that is false. Some would want to restrict that knowing to only those things that are possible to know.
- **Omnipresent** – God is not limited by either space or time.
- **All loving** – God is love.
- **Perfectly good** – God is morally perfect.

4 Are the attributes self-consistent?

For the concept of God to have meaning, the attributes proposed must be self-consistent and consistent with one another. A lack of self-consistency would mean that the concept was incoherent and therefore meaningless. It might be argued that we cannot know what God is like, as God is transcendent. Even if that is true and God can only be known by revelation, what we believe about God still has to make sense to us. If what is believed is not understood or doesn't make sense, then it is hard to see how there is any content to the belief.

Philosophers have challenged several of the attributes outlined above on the grounds that the concept is contradictory or incoherent.

a) Eternal

The idea of God being timeless is a concept that has taxed many a philosopher. The classical view argued for by philosophers such as Augustine, Anselm and Aquinas sees God as outside of time. God sees all things as eternally present. Aquinas used the illustration of someone sitting on a hill watching people walking below. The view of the walkers is that of people in front, beside and behind them; in other words a particular spatial order. However, the observer on the hill is outside of that spatial order yet observes all the order in one view. Similarly God could see all time in one view. Another illustration Aquinas used was of a circle where the centre point represents eternity and the circumference represents time. Likewise Augustine took the view that the author of the space-time continuum could not be bound by it.

More recent support for this view of God outside of time has come from the theory of Special Relativity. K. Rogers (*Perfect Being Theology*, 2000) explains:

> If time is relative to particular observational frameworks, then there is no absolute, universal time which would encompass God and the physical world.
>
> *Perfect Being Theology* (2000), p. 56

However, many regard such a concept of God outside of time as self-contradictory or incoherent. It is argued that the theory of Special Relativity actually argues for an absolute and universal time for the entire physical universe. There is still a lively debate among physicists about the nature of time, or even whether it exists. It would be unwise to be dogmatic on this issue.

More traditional rejections of God outside of time involve the claim that our thoughts and desires are all performed in the present with reference to the past and future, and they take time. However, the claim of timelessness for God demands that all of God's actions and thoughts and desires take place simultaneously. There is only the 'now' for a God who is timeless. Such things as remembering or acting seem impossible for a God who is timeless. How could God act in particular events in history such as the parting of the Red Sea, since it would seem to require Him to enter a time frame? In particular the creation of a universe is problematic if there is no time frame in God Himself – for there has to be a time when God decides to bring the universe into being and a time when there was no universe. In other words it is not at all clear what it means to say that God acts 'timelessly' in time. For the Christian, the issue is particularly problematic since it makes the claim that God became man and entered human history. Swinburne (*Is There a God?*, 1996) concludes:

> I prefer the understanding of God being eternal as His being everlasting rather than as His being timeless. (p. 9)

However, to claim that God is bounded by time also gives rise to charges of incoherency. If God exists in time, then His past and future would limit His present.

b) Omnipotent

Philosophers do not generally regard the idea that God cannot do the logically impossible, or perform acts that are inconsistent with His nature, as a limitation of His power. Hence it is argued that God cannot make square circles and God cannot sin. In a sense, God not doing the logically impossible can be seen as a reflection of His nature, since it would mean He would do something contrary to reason.

However, many argue that omnipotence is self-contradictory. The classic attacks on this concept have been expressed by means of paradoxes:

- The paradox of the stone shows there are things God cannot do. The paradox is stated in the question 'Can God create a stone that He cannot lift?' If He can create the stone, then He lacks power to lift it, but if He cannot create such a stone, then He also lacks power. Various attempts have been made to find a solution to remove the apparent contradiction. The most favoured response points out that it is a logical impossibility for God to create a stone He cannot lift, since He is all-powerful. Hence it does not detract from His omnipotence.
- Another paradox is whether God can create a creature whose will is so free that God cannot control it. One resolution to this problem is to argue that it is logically impossible for a choice to be both free and controlled at the same time.
- Another paradox is whether God has the power to change the past. The implication is that the past cannot be changed and therefore God is not all-powerful. Once again the appeal to logical impossibilities resounds. If the past is changed, then it ceases to be the past.

It could also be questioned whether omnipotence is a necessary attribute of God. God may choose to limit His divine power in the interests of love, but in that case He does remain all-powerful, unless He cedes His power permanently.

c) Omniscient

Omniscience is the ability to know everything. Philosophers point out a possible incoherency if it is also claimed that God makes decisions. God can't know His own decisions while He is making them, yet if God is omniscient, He would know all things including those decisions. This seems a contradiction. One solution is to say that God makes those decisions outside of time. In other words, as God is timeless, He sees the past, present and future, all in the same moment.

d) Omnipresent

Omnipresence should not be confused with the idea of 'God in everything', which is more akin to pantheism. But if God is a person, how can He be everywhere? Aquinas resolved this dilemma by stating that God's presence 'everywhere' meant there was unlimited scope for God's operative powers. In other words, God affects everything. This shows how important it is to define terms. Clear definition may help remove apparent contradictions.

e) All-loving

It is difficult to define a state of 'all-loving'. Some philosophers argue that love has no limits. This is expressed by the phrase 'love has no intrinsic maximum' (see ontological argument, p. 21).

f) Perfectly good

Perhaps a stronger problem revolves around the question of the relation between goodness and God. What is the source of the standard of moral goodness? Is God the source of moral goodness, or is there a standard of goodness to which God is subject to conform? This dilemma is not new and can be found in Plato's *Euthyphro*.

If God is almighty, how can there be a source of moral authority over and above Himself?

The classical answer to the dilemma has been to support the view that God is the source of moral goodness. The modern philosopher William Alston concluded:

We can think of God Himself, the individual being, as the supreme standard of goodness.

Divine Nature and Human Language (1989), p. 268

Such an approach accepts human moral duty to obey what God commands but denies that God must conform to some external source of values. Rather God Himself is the standard.

5 Are the attributes consistent with one another?

Besides the need for self-consistency for the attributes of God, there is also a requirement that the attributes are consistent with one another.

a) Omnipotent, omniscient, creator and perfectly good

These four attributes of God would seemingly make the existence of evil an impossibility. (For a full discussion of this issue see Chapter 11.)

b) Eternal, omniscient and free/responsible

How can God know the future, since it has not yet been decided? The concept is full of difficulties. If God does know the future, some would argue it implies there are no acts of free will, since He knows what will happen. Alternatively, if God doesn't know the future, then He is not omniscient.

Others argue that the fact that God knows the future doesn't therefore necessitate Him over-riding my free will. He merely knows what free choice I make. Though I am in time, God is outside of time. A famous attempt at a solution was proposed by Luis de Molina (1536—1600). Molina maintained that God would know what people would freely choose to do in all circumstances where some choice was available. This included choices that were hypothetical in that either the person or the circumstances never came into being. Such knowledge was termed '**middle knowledge**'.

In contrast, Swinburne rejects the view of God as outside of time and argues that God only knows that which it is logically possible to know. This then excludes events that God permits that are the result of free will choices by humans. Such events God would not know, but supporters of this view do not regard it as a loss of omniscience.

Certainly the problem has been recognised for centuries and a good discussion can be found in G Hughes' article 'Omniscience', in B Davies (ed), *Philosophy of Religion, A Guide to the Subject*, pp. 86–94.

6 Recent developments

In recent times there has been a challenge to the traditional debate about the concept of God. Theologians like Don Cupitt have questioned the whole notion of God as a real, external, objective being. Cupitt argues that God is just a symbol for the religious and spiritual life. In his book *Taking Leave of God* (1980), Cupitt states:

> I do not suppose God to be an objectified individual over and above the religious requirement. (p. 85)

Indeed Cupitt offers a new definition of 'God'. In this new way of understanding religion,

> God is Christian spirituality in coded form, for God is a symbol that represents to us everything that spirituality requires of us and promises to us. (p. 14)

Modern linguistic philosophy has tended to insist that we need to define our terms first, before investigating their place in the real world. We can define God in any way we like, but we are not having a meaningful debate unless those in dispute have an agreed definition of the being whose existence they are considering. In other words we can only debate the existence of God if we have an agreed definition of God. In a similar way we can only debate the issue of whether the moon is made of green cheese if we have an agreed understanding of what we mean by the moon. Otherwise debate is literally meaningless.

Cupitt's definition of God would mean that the traditional concepts of God would be understood in a very different way. Omnipotence, for example, would:

> not refer to the power of a creator God, but to the power inherent in each one of us if we would give up living for ourselves and instead devote ourselves to others.
>
> P Vardy, *The Puzzle of God* (1990), p. 120

Answering questions on Chapter 2

A typical exam question on this area might ask you to 'identify and briefly describe two of God's properties'. Note that there are two trigger words that need to be addressed. Candidates would be expected to identify appropriate attributes and also provide an accurate description of what each attribute entails. At AS and A2 level the answers are marked according to level descriptors. These level descriptors are available from the exam board and it is essential that candidates acquire a copy. For instance, if only one property was fully identified and described or if both properties were identified but not described, then it would not be possible to gain a top-level mark, however much the candidate wrote. Candidates still have a tendency to equate quantity with quality.

Another question area might ask candidates to 'explain the philosophical problems that arise when combining two or more of God's properties'. This is what is called an AO1 skill because what is being asked for is knowledge and understanding. However, many candidates read it as an evaluative skill and so engage in a detailed critical assessment. But the question does not actually ask candidates to resolve the problems, merely to identify them. Hence, no marks would be awarded for the critical assessment aspect of the answer.

It is important to know which assessment objectives are being tested. Knowledge and understanding questions often use such trigger words as:

- Define
- Describe
- Examine
- Explain
- Identify
- Outline
- Select

The Exam Board issues mark schemes for every exam. These are very useful documents as they are the means by which Principal Examiners communicate common errors and weaknesses in exam answers. They also make clear the standard expected and the type of material that might achieve that standard.

3 The existence of God – I

theism – the belief in a personal deity, creator of everything that exists and who is distinct from that creation

a priori – prior to experience

a posteriori – from experience

necessary being – a being whose non-existence would be a self-contradiction. This is its sense in the Ontological Argument. It can also be used in the causal sense, of a being who is required as an explanation

analytic – a statement where the predicate is contained in the subject

synthetic – a statement where the predicate is not contained in the subject

contingent – that which need not be, that which could have been different; something that has dependency

modal – the modal in which something occurs, e.g. either necessary or possible

possible world – anything that can be conceived of, or is logically consistent

1 Introduction

> **KEY ISSUE** There are five classical, **theistic** proofs.

Four of the theistic proofs attempt to demonstrate the existence of God from some observation or experience of the universe. These are:

- The **Cosmological Argument**, which infers God from the existence of the world or from phenomena within it, such as causality.
- The **Teleological Argument**, which infers a designer from the occurrence of order and regularity in the world.
- The **Moral Argument**, which infers God as the explanation for moral consciousness or the guarantor for the highest good.
- The **Religious Experience Argument**, which sees God as the best explanation for experiences that people claim that are beyond the normal.

Because these all involve claims about the world that can be investigated empirically (by the senses) or be verified by experience, they are called *a posteriori* arguments. Thus they contain premises that are based on experience, such as order in the world or moral consciousness.

In contrast the fifth argument is *a priori*. Such premises are prior to any experience of the world, and are not verified by experience. This argument for the existence of God is:

● The **Ontological Argument** which concludes that God's definition entails His existence.

As we look at each of the arguments in turn, it will be clear that each comes in a variety of versions. I have selected the key versions, but in your supplementary reading you may well come across other approaches. Added to this is the problem that not all philosophers actually agree how to interpret the proofs, since their views about the meaning of the word 'God', for instance, will affect their interpretations. We will return to the issue of the value of the proofs after we have considered the individual theistic proofs.

Traditionally, the arguments have all been regarded as deductive and flawed. However, in more recent years the *a posteriori* arguments have been presented as inductive and are assessed in terms of persuasiveness. Swinburne in particular has taken this approach in his book *The Existence of God* (1979). The cumulative approach in considering all the arguments together as persuasive of God's existence is another trend of last century.

We will consider first the one argument that has remained deductive in its form.

2 The Ontological Argument

a) Historical background

'Ontological' literally means 'concerned with being'. This argument was most classically propounded by Anselm (1033–1109), who became Archbishop of Canterbury and is a canonised saint of the Roman Catholic church. The actual argument can be found in chapters 2–4 of Anselm's *Proslogion* (1077–78). The argument was sharply criticised in his own time, and centuries later by such people as Aquinas and Immanuel Kant. Among those who have supported it are Descartes, and more recently Malcolm and Plantinga. This argument appeals more to those who already believe in God than to the atheist. Scholars seem divided as to whether Anselm meant the argument to be effective to the atheist.

As we have noted above, the argument differs from all other proofs in being *a priori* (prior to experience) since it proceeds from the idea of God – instead of arguing *a posteriori* (based on experience), i.e. from some feature of the universe. As an *a priori* argument it has as its ground a logical demonstration that either totally succeeds or totally fails.

Its scope is greater than that of the other arguments since they can give only a limited view of what God is like, while the concept of God as 'the most perfect being' implies a whole range of other qualities.

b) Anselm's argument

i) First form

Anselm began by defining God as 'a being than which nothing greater can be conceived'. However, if it is the greatest, then it must be something more than merely existing in people's thoughts. We can think of something greater than a mere idea. If God is the greatest, He must really exist separately from people's thoughts. He must exist actually, in reality.

As a formal deductive argument it is:

- God is the greatest possible being (nothing greater can be conceived).
- If God exists in the mind alone (only as an idea), then a greater being could be imagined to exist both in the mind and in reality.
- This being would then be greater than God.
- Thus God cannot exist only as an idea in the mind.

Therefore, God exists both in the mind (as an idea) and in reality.

In summary, it is self-contradictory to be able to conceive of something than which nothing greater can be thought and yet to deny that that something exists.

ii) Second form

Anselm developed his argument to demonstrate that it was impossible to conceive of God as not existing. This is the idea that God is eternal and has always been, so He is not limited by, or in, time. Put another way, Anselm argued that God had necessary existence: He could not not be. The reason is that this state is greater than a being who comes and goes out of existence. As a deductive argument it is:

- God is the greatest possible being (nothing greater can be conceived).
- It is greater to be a **necessary being** (cannot not be) than a contingent being (can cease to exist).
- If God exists only as a contingent being so can therefore be imagined not to exist, then a greater being could be imagined that cannot be conceived not to exist.
- This being would then be greater than God.
- God is therefore a necessary being.

Therefore God must exist in reality.

In summary, God must be a necessary being, meaning, He cannot not exist. Necessary here means logical necessity. It would be a logical contradiction to claim that God does not exist, since any being who has the property of necessary existence could not fail to exist.

The Ontological Argument claims to reveal that inherent in the concept of God is necessary existence. When you come to analyse and examine the concept of God, it becomes clear that existence is part of the concept. Such propositions are called **analytic** and have the property that the predicate is contained in the subject. The predicate is that which is said about the subject. An example of an analytic sentence is 'All bachelors are single.' Thus 'all bachelors' is the subject and 'being single' is the predicate. As you can see, an analytic statement does not contain any new information but clarifies the term. The surprise that the Ontological Argument claims to reveal is that existence is part of the concept of God. We refer to propositions that are analytic and about existence as *analytic existential propositions*. Hence 'God exists' is claimed to be an example of such a proposition.

Analytic statements can be true or false. The proposition 'All bachelors are married' is analytic but false. It is analytic because the married state is part of the concept of 'bachelor'. The fact that it is analytic does not tell you whether it is true or false, but merely how to decide whether it is true or false. The way to decide is by considering the meaning of the words.

In passing it should be noted that a sentence such as 'The cat sat on the mat' is clearly not an analytic statement, since there is nothing in the analysis of the concept of 'cat' that contains the idea of 'sitting on the mat'! Statements like these that add new information are called **synthetic**. Their truth value (i.e. whether they are true or false) is determined by empirical evidence.

c) Supporters of the Ontological Argument

i) Descartes (1596–1650)

Descartes is regarded as the founder of modern philosophy. In *Meditations* he proposed his philosophical arguments for a unified and certain body of human knowledge. He broke free from the dogmas of Aristotle and supported instead the new age of science. Descartes favoured independent enquiry from first principles and asserted only that which could be known to be certain. A crucial part of his argument involved the existence of God as a guarantor for the certainty that the external world exists. The argument he uses is a form of the Ontological Argument:

● God, a supremely perfect being, has all perfections.
● Existence is a perfection.

Therefore God, a supremely perfect being, exists.

In *Meditation 5*, Descartes argued that there were some qualities that an object necessarily had or else it would not be that object. He considered a triangle that must have three angles adding up to 180 degrees. Equally the notion of a hill demands the idea of a valley. In the same way, existence cannot be separated from the concept of God.

d) Recent reformulations

In the twentieth century the ontological argument enjoyed a revival. Both Norman Malcolm in *Philosophical Review 69* (1960), and Charles Hartshorne in *The Logic of Perfection* (La Salle, 1962), have centred their arguments on the idea of necessary existence. They describe it as existence which cannot be brought about nor threatened by anything. Thus God's existence is either impossible or necessary. It cannot be impossible since the concept is not self-contradictory. Therefore God necessarily exists.

Alvin Plantinga in *The Nature of Necessity* (Oxford, 1974), has reformulated the argument using the concept of **possible worlds**. The idea of possible worlds is a popular method used by philosophers to determine the modality (necessity, impossibility or possibility) of statements. Hence this formulation of the Ontological Argument has become known as the **modal** form. To test for logical impossibility, these philosophers ask us to think of a possible world in which the statement is true. If you can, then the statement is not logically impossible. For a statement to be logically necessary it would have to be true in all possible worlds. So the argument goes as follows:

● There is a possible world, in which there exists a being with maximal greatness (existing in every possible world) and excellence (having the properties of omniscience, omnipotence, etc.).
● Therefore: In any possible world this being has maximal excellence (omniscience, omnipotence, etc.).
● Our world is a possible world (since our world exists).

Therefore: In our world there is this being!

e) Criticisms of the ontological argument

As for the arguments supporting the Ontological Argument, there are a number of different criticisms.

i) The definition of God

This criticism argues that we do not know what the word 'God' means, or at any rate the meaning is not clear. That is why Aquinas never supported the Ontological Argument. He felt that such arguments for God had to be causal, based on effects that you could see, and from them deduce that a God was required to cause them.

However, most argue that the definition that Anselm used is not nonsense. It does convey meaning.

Another similar criticism argues that the definition of God is wrong. Anselm's definition is not what people see God as. However, whatever one believes about God, it seems reasonable to say that nothing can be thought to be greater than God.

Perhaps a stronger criticism concerns the idea of the 'greatest or most perfect being'. Do we really have a concept of this? Indeed, is it a meaningful concept or is it like the concept of 'greatest number'? Does the property of 'most loving' have a maximum?

ii) Logical tricks

The Ontological Argument attempts to pass from the thought of the existence of a thing to the actual existence of that thing. Many argue that you cannot move from a concept to reality itself, but merely to a concept of reality (see (v)).

The argument also begs the question since it makes the existence of God 'true by definition'. In addition, Malcolm's argument commits the fallacy of equivocation. This fallacy occurs when a word is used in two different senses. The word misused by Malcolm is 'impossible'. He is accused of using it both in the sense of a matter of fact (unable to come about) and also in the sense of being logically contradictory. Malcolm concludes in his argument that God is necessary in the former sense (factual) whereas He is 'necessary' in the latter sense (logical). As a result, what the argument does show is that *if* God exists, then God exists necessarily, but not *that* God exists.

Plantinga's argument merely shows that God is possible, *not* that he is actual. Others point out that if you can have a being with maximal greatness and excellence, then what results from arguing for a possible world where no being exemplifies maximal greatness?

Perhaps an even more radical criticism is to disagree with the proposition that to deny that God exists involves a self-contradiction, on the basis that logic is purely an arbitrary linguistic convention that tells us nothing about reality.

iii) Existence is not a great-making quality

One of the major opponents of the Ontological Argument was Immanuel Kant. He made the point that existence is not a real predicate. That is, it does not tell us what an object is like (i.e. some quality or characteristic). Kant felt that 'exist' was a word that merely stated that a concept had an actuality. It did not actually add anything to the concept. The real contains no more than the merely possible, so a concept is not made greater by adding reality.

Kant expressed it like this, in his book *The Critique of Pure Reason* (1781):

> If we take the subject (God) with all its predicates (e.g. all knowledge), and say 'God is' or 'There is a God', we attach no new predicate to the concept of God ... merely posit it as being an object that stands in relation to my concept. The content of both must be one and the same ... The real contains no more than the merely possible. A hundred real thalers do not contain the least coin more than a hundred possible thalers.

(NB A thaler was an old German silver coin.)

Brian Davies in *Thinking about God* (1985) has expressed the same point using a different example:

> For someone who claims to compare two things, one of which exists and the other of which does not, is just not doing what he says he is doing. If we contrast (or compare) A with B, then both A and B must exist. A non-existent book is not different from a real book. Nor is it similar. It is just not there to be either similar or different to anything. Hence as Kant said 'Being' is the positing of a thing.

We do not add anything to the concept when we declare that it 'is'. Otherwise it would not be exactly the same thing that exists but something more than we had thought in the concept; and we could not, therefore, say that the exact object of my concept exists.

Thus many regard 'exists' more as a number. To say that something exists is to deny the number zero. Bertrand Russell made a similar point. He used the example of 'cows exist' but 'unicorns do not exist'. He said that we are not talking about cows and saying that they have the attribute of existence or that unicorns lack this attribute. Rather we are talking of the concepts of a cow and a unicorn and saying that one of them has an instance and one of them does not.

It was because Malcolm felt that existence was not a great-making quality that he was led to develop his form of the Ontological Argument based more closely on Anselm's second form. Malcolm argued that necessary being is a property, namely the property of an inability to be generated or made corrupt.

However, supporters of the Ontological Argument have responded to such criticisms, arguing that existence can be a real predicate. Stephen Davis (*God, Reason and Theistic Proofs*, 1997) notes that:

> Of the real hundred thalers, my concept of them includes the property of having-purchasing-power-in-the-real-world. My concept of a hundred thalers does not have that property.

iv) You cannot have an analytic existential proposition

We defined an analytic proposition on page 19. An analytic existential proposition is an analytic statement about existence. Many philosophers argue that propositions about existence are not analytic but synthetic and **contingent**. If this is correct, then the Ontological

Argument has been guilty of some logical tricks since its conclusion appears to be an existential analytic statement, namely 'God exists'.

In reply, supporters of the Ontological Argument have argued that it *is* possible to have analytic existential propositions. They cite such examples as 'A number greater than a million exists' and 'Science Fiction characters do not exist' as analytic existential propositions. The debate continues … !

v) You cannot define things into existence

Even if one were to accept that existence was a great-making property, some philosophers still feel that the argument fails. This is because the thrust of the Ontological Argument seems to be that by defining God you can be assured of His existence. To most, such an idea seems absurd. It implies you can define anything into existence. There seems to be some intellectual sleight of hand involved in moving from a definition to proving an existence.

Many feel that 'filling out a concept' and 'showing that there really is something to which the concept refers', are two quite different processes and that the first does *not* lead to the second. Remember that the Ontological Argument alleges that we cannot explain the concept of God properly without coming to the conclusion that He exists.

This apparent flaw in the argument was noted by a monk called Gaunilo, at the time of Anselm. He used the illustration of a 'lost island' that was the most excellent of all islands. He argued that though he could easily form the concept in his mind, it would be absurd to conclude therefore that such an island existed in reality. The thrust of the argument is that if the existence of God can be proved in this way, then the existence of anything (such as a lost island) can also be proved.

In reply, Anselm argued that islands are contingent and therefore do not have necessary existence as an aspect of their properties. However, God does. Indeed, God is unique in this aspect. Existence is not part of the greatness of an island, whereas necessary existence is part of the concept of God. Hence to say that 'God does not exist' is the same thing as saying 'An existing God does not exist'. Such a statement is nonsense. The reason why the above is nonsense is that contradiction results from negating the predicate of a true analytic statement.

Kant proposed that no such contradiction arose if you rejected both subject and predicate, 'for nothing is left that you can contradict.' Kant expressed it in these words (*Critique of Pure Reason*, trans. N Kempsmith, New York: St Martins Press, 1965):

> It would be self-contradictory to posit a triangle and yet reject its three angles, but there is no contradiction in rejecting the triangle together with its three angles.

Thus if we were to look again at Gaunilo's criticism of Anselm, then he appears to be saying that it is not a contradiction to claim that there is not a being who in reality exists that has the property of necessary existence.

Definitions only tell us what God would be like *if* He existed. It cannot establish whether He does in fact exist. One can move from a concept of imagination to a concept of reality but not from a concept of imagination to reality. Hence there is no contradiction in denying the reality of a conceptual being who has necessary existence.

When we say that existence is part of God's definition, we are merely saying that no non-existing being can be God. To put it another way, if God exists He will have necessary existence, but it is not a contradiction to say that such a concept does not have an actuality.

Hume said in *Dialogues Concerning Natural Religion* that:

> However much our concept of an object may contain, we must go outside of it to determine whether or not it exists. We cannot define something into existence – even if it has all the perfections we can imagine.

As you may have guessed, this view has not gone unchallenged. Some people have pointed out that explaining a concept can make non-existence apparent. Take, for example, 'round squares'. These cannot exist. A concept leads to a non-existence. So perhaps the two processes of concept and actuality are related and therefore *perhaps* it is possible that by filling out a concept you can move to actuality. All is very teasing, and hence the debate continues.

f) Conclusions

It seems that the Ontological Argument is insufficient to convert the atheist, since it seems to fail as a proof. However, perhaps that was not its original intention. It is likely that Anselm was writing for those who already had a belief in God, and thus to show that their faith was rational. Indeed, he says in the preface to his *Proslogion*:

> I have written the following treatise in the person of one who … seeks to understand what he believes …

At best one can say that if God exists, He will have necessary existence, *but* perhaps that does not prove that He does exist.

A new development in the ontological debate involves seeing God *not* as an object but rather as a grammatical observation. This new approach will be discussed in Chapter 9. One thing does seem certain – the last word has yet to be said about the Ontological Argument.

Answering questions on Chapter 3

Usually examiners ask questions focused on some formulation on the Ontological Argument and some assessment of that argument. A particular proponent of the argument, such as Anselm, may be requested. Consider the following:

1. Outline the Ontological Argument for the existence of God and consider the view that, while it may strengthen a believer's faith, it has no value for the non-believer.
2. **a)** Examine and assess the view that the Ontological Argument for the existence of God is convincing. **b)** In what respects is the Ontological Argument different from *a posteriori* arguments?
3. How successfully do the Ontological Argument and the argument from experience counter the claim that God exists only in the mind?

Clearly none of the above questions allow a 'write all you know' answer. Each question has a particular focus. Selecting material to addresses that focus is the art of passing exams.

Question 1 links the Ontological Argument to the issue of its value, particularly in respect to the believer and non-believer. Just listing the various critiques against the Ontological Argument would gain few marks. Question 2 requires knowledge of *a priori* and *a posteriori*. Again note the key word *different*. A contrast needs to be made using the Ontological Argument.

Often one argument for the existence of God is compared or linked with another, as in question 3. It is always a good idea to plan essays and use the key words in the question as the basis of the plan. Questions usually contain trigger words to indicate the type of analysis that is wanted. For instance:

- **Assess** – argue both for and against and indicate a conclusion.
- **Compare** – look for similarities and differences between.
- **Contrast** – set in opposition in order to bring out the differences.
- **Contribute** – situation before; what new element has it added; evaluate.
- **Discuss** – examine by argument, sift and debate, giving reasons pro and con.
- **Evaluate** – make an appraisal of the worth of something, in the light of its truth; support by discussion of evidence which is critically assessed.
- **How far** – critically evaluate; weigh the evidence and come to a view.

The existence of God – 2

KEYWORDS

contingent – that which need not be, that which could have been different; something that has dependency

cosmology – the study of the nature and order of the universe

Big-Bang Theory – the theory that the universe had a beginning in a definite moment in time

Oscillating Universe Theory – the theory that there have been an infinite series of expanding and contracting universes

1 The Cosmological Argument

a) Historical background

The Cosmological Argument attempts to infer the existence of God from the existence of the cosmos or from phenomena within it. The claim is that the universe cannot account for its own existence and so this argument seeks causes that have their solution in the existence of a God. It is an argument that has a long history. In *Timaeus*, Plato says that every created thing must be created by some cause. The argument is also found in Aristotle's works. Aquinas presented the popular form in the first three of his 'Five Ways'. Further support was given by Descartes and Leibniz. In his book *Theodicy* (1710), Leibniz said that the great principle of the Cosmological Argument is that 'nothing takes place without sufficient reason'. Its modern

Figure 1 - Thomas Aquinas (1225–1274)

proponents who argue that it has some degree of probability are Craig and Swinburne. Its main opponents have been Hume and Kant.

b) Aquinas' arguments

St Thomas Aquinas (1225–1274) has been a very influential philosopher and theologian who is especially highly regarded by Roman Catholics. He lived at a time when a renewed interest in Aristotle coincided with a view that philosophy could be useful to Christian theology, to demonstrate the reasonableness of faith and also to help explore articles of faith. Hence Aquinas attempted to apply the philosophy of Aristotle to Christianity. The philosophy of Aquinas is often referred to by the name 'Thomism'. He wrote prolifically and in *Summa Theologica*, a book containing over 4000 pages, Aquinas devoted only two pages to his arguments for the existence of God. However, their compact form has made them popular, and they have become known as the Five Ways.

- The Unmoved Mover.
- The Uncaused Causer.
- Possibility and Necessity.
- Goodness, Truth and Nobility.
- Teleological.

These five arguments are all *a posteriori* and have as their starting point some observation or experience of the universe. The first three 'ways' are different variations of the Cosmological Argument.

i) The First Way – The Unmoved Mover (The Unchanged Changer/ The Prime Mover)

There are various types of motion (change): change of place, change of size and change of state. It is the last one that Aquinas had particularly in mind. Here movement has the sense of moving from potentiality to actuality. For instance, wood is potentially hot, and for a piece of wood to become hot it has to be changed by fire. What is potentially x is not actually x, yet the actually x can only be produced by something that is actually x. Whatever is moved (changed) must be moved (changed) by another, which itself was moved (changed). If we trace back we must arrive at a first mover, moved by no other. This is what we understand to be God. Expressed formally:

- Everything that is in motion (change) is moved (changed) by something else.
- Infinite regress is impossible.

Therefore there must be a first mover (changer).

Aquinas was not arguing that the universe necessarily had a beginning. He thought it did, but said that you could not reason that out as it was revealed doctrine. Rather his emphasis was on dependency. This dependency argument is one that has reappeared in the twentieth century and is taken up by Swinburne. Christian theology has always taught that God sustains the universe. In other words, if God ceased to exist then the universe would also cease. Therefore there must be an initiator of the change whose continued existence is depended upon. In the same way, a play depends on the continued existence of actors. This type of causal relationship is what Aquinas had in mind.

ii) The Second Way – The Uncaused Causer (The First Cause Argument)
This follows a similar line of argument but replaces motion (change) with cause:

● Every effect has a cause.
● Infinite regress is impossible.

Therefore there must be a first cause.

In other words, everything that happens has a cause. The cause itself has a cause. Something cannot cause itself for this would mean it preceded itself and this is impossible. Hence the need for an uncaused causer, namely God.

One of the differences between these two 'ways' is that in the first, attention is centred on the fact that things are acted upon, whereas in the second, the attention is on things as agents (doing the acting upon). The first cause sees God as a factual necessity, as the causal explanation to the universe. This means that God is seen as a being who is not dependent on any other for His existence. He is a contingent being that is causeless, and it would not be a logical contradiction if such a being did not actually exist. This is in contrast to the Ontological Argument that sees God as a logically necessary being. Remember that in the case of a logically necessary being, it would be a logical contradiction to claim that it did not exist.

iii) The Third Way – Possibility and Necessity (Contingency)
For Aquinas, anything that had a property was referred to as a 'being'. The world consists of **contingent** items, that is, beings that are generated and perish (see page 26). If all beings were contingent, then at one time nothing would have existed. This is because there would have been a time prior to the coming into existence of contingent beings. But if that is the case, then nothing would be able to come into existence as everything contingent has a prior cause. Thus all beings cannot be contingent. There must exist a necessary being which Aquinas refers to as God. Again, expressed formally:

● Some contingent beings exist.
● If any contingent beings exist then a necessary being must exist.

Therefore a necessary being exists, namely God.

c) Criticisms of Aquinas' arguments

- Some scholars have argued that Aquinas' arguments rest on assumptions that are no longer widely held. Ancient and medieval science thought in terms of a hierarchy of causes, which is different to modern-day thinking. It is an assumption that actual x can only be brought about by what is actual x. For example, two cold objects rubbed together will cause heat.
- Why cannot there be an endless series of causes? In reply Mackie (*The Miracle of Theism*, 1982, p. 90) cites the analogy of a railway train consisting of an infinite number of carriages. Each carriage may move the next carriage but ultimately it only makes sense if there is an engine. The problem then becomes one of demonstrating that Aquinas' Three Ways have such a relation of dependence.
- Why cannot there be some contingent items that have lasted through all past time and will show their contingency by perishing at some time in the future?
- If nothing can cause itself, how can God be seen as an uncaused causer? In reply it is stated that the cause of the universe must lie in something outside it. Thus Aquinas did not see God as just another thing like everything else in the universe, but bigger. Rather, God is of a totally different order and not subject to the same conditions as the universe.
- Why a single termination? Why must the regress lead to one first cause? Independent happenings might lead back to causes which are independent of each other. Therefore there would not be a single first cause but a plurality of first causes.
- Why cannot the different forms of the Three Ways lead to a different 'God' for each? Why should it lead to God as understood in the Christian concept? Indeed, why should God not be the originator and now no longer exist? After all, a mother causes a child but then dies.
- The argument begins with 'this world' and concludes with concepts of which we have no experience, e.g. uncaused, infinity.
- The universe is not contingent, i.e. matter or energy in the universe is eternal. Particular objects come and go, but the matter of which they are composed is forever and exists necessarily. It could not have failed to exist. There is not a reason – it is just brute fact. Thus the great ultimates of the universe are about matter, not about a metaphysical being called God.
- In reply it is argued that since everything in the universe is contingent, everything could cease to exist simultaneously, and then the universe itself would cease. But if it can cease to exist, then it must be contingent. Recent thinking in physics has also questioned the eternal nature of matter.

d) Other forms of the Cosmological Argument

i) The Principle of Sufficient Reason
Leibniz (1646–1716) avoided the problem of infinite regression by reinterpreting the endless series, not of events, but of explanations. Even if the universe had always existed, there is nothing within the universe to show *why* it exists. According to Leibniz, everything has a sufficient reason.

The Principle of Sufficient Reason states that, in the case of any positive truth, there is some sufficient reason for it, i.e. there is some sort of explanation, known or unknown, for everything. The world does not seem to contain within itself the reason for its own existence. Therefore God exists.

Hume (1711–1776) argued that it was illegitimate to move from saying that every event in the universe has a cause to the claim that the universe has a cause. Bertrand Russell made a similar point by remarking that this was like moving from saying that every human being has a mother to the claim that the human race as a whole has a mother. One cannot move from individual causes to the claim that the totality has a cause.

In his book *Why I am not a Christian* (1957, p. 140) Russell says 'the universe is just there, and that's all there is to say'. However, we ask 'why' of things within the universe, therefore it seems consistent to ask why the universe itself is there. The theist assumes that the universe is intelligible and ultimately depends on an eternal self-existent reality. Copleston likened Russell's approach of denying the problem to saying 'If one refuses to even sit down at the chess board and make a move, one cannot, of course, be checkmated.'

ii) The beginning argument
People often say that 'things cannot have got going by themselves'. This argument can be called 'the beginning argument', and is sometimes referred to as the Kalam Cosmological Argument, popular in Islam. Its origins date back to about 850 CE to a group which belonged to the Islamic Kalam tradition of philosophy. However, the argument was used by John Locke (1632-1704) and has had a revival in the late twentieth century, mainly through the writings of William Craig.

This argument claims that everything that begins to exist has a cause of its existence, and since the universe began to exist, the universe has a cause of its existence. Transcending the entire universe there exists a cause which brought the universe into being. This cause is God.

Attempts have been made to destroy the argument by claiming that it is possible to imagine something coming into existence without a cause. However, you can only know whether something began to exist if it has a cause. If not, how do you know it did not exist elsewhere?

Support for something without a cause has recently come from subatomic physics. Here it appears that electrons can pass out of existence at one point and then come back into existence elsewhere without any cause. In reply, some argue that this phenomenon results from the limits of our investigative equipment, i.e. our present scientific knowledge stops us finding the cause, but there is one.

The main debate therefore tends to revolve around the assumption that the universe had a beginning. Certainly modern cosmology suggests the **Big-Bang Theory** which implies a finite past history of the universe, even if it does not imply finite time. Support for such a theory includes the evidence that the universe is expanding, which suggests that it had a starting point.

Philosophically speaking, if the universe had no beginning, then an actual infinite number of past moments of the universe's history have elapsed, and they are being added to as time goes on. But one cannot add to an infinite number of things. For instance, if there is an infinite number of dogs, then one cannot add to that number of dogs by introducing another dog. Likewise, if there has elapsed an infinite number of past moments of the universe, then this number cannot be added to either. Yet the universe continues to exist. Moments continue to be added. This implies that the universe had a beginning. Further, if the universe had no beginning, then an infinity of years will have been traversed, which is impossible.

Needless to say, the above arguments have been challenged. For example, it is argued that:

- Modern cosmology allows for an infinite past history of the universe since it is consistent with the evidence to have an infinite series of expanding and contracting universes. This is known as the **Oscillating Universe Theory**.
- Many argue that it is to misunderstand the word 'infinity' to treat it as though it were a number. Rather it is a concept. Hence it is meaningless to speak of 'adding more moments of time' or 'traversing infinite years'.
- If there were no starting point, then from any specific point in past time there is only a finite stretch that needs to be traversed to reach the present.

Given that the universe had a beginning, some philosophers question whether God must be the cause. Even if God did start it, God could then cease to be. This is very far from the traditional view that God not only began the world but sustains it, and that without God things would cease to be.

e) Conclusions

The Cosmological Argument does not force the atheist to become a theist, since the atheist can still claim that the universe has no ultimate explanation but is just a brute fact. Hence it can only point to the *possibility* of God. It does bring into sharp contrast the two ways of looking at the universe – namely that it is inexplicable or that it is intelligible. If there is an explanation, it is possible that it could be contained in 'God'.

Answering questions on Chapter 4

Often in exam questions, the issue of proof is required to be discussed. It is therefore important to be aware of the different shades of meaning of 'proof' that were discussed in Chapter 1. Examiners often link together two arguments for the existence of God so that students can compare and contrast their structure and success as arguments. Consider the following:

1. Outline the Cosmological Argument for the existence of God and assess its claim to prove that God exists.
2. **a)** Outline the Cosmological and Design Arguments for the existence of God. **b)** Choose one of these arguments and examine criticisms that have been made of its form, content and conclusions.
3. **a)** Discuss how a coherent explanation of the universe might be provided by both of the following arguments for the existence of God: (i) cosmological (ii) design. **b)** Select one of the arguments and consider reasons why it may not, by itself, offer such a coherent explanation.

Note that the questions demand knowledge of more than one argument. Also, examiners are not expecting all variations of the Cosmological Argument. It would be sufficient to deal with one in depth rather than just to briefly list all of them. A similar approach is required when evaluating. Avoid just listing criticisms. Evaluation at a simple level is commenting about the views presented. That includes reflecting or responding to those arguments and so discussing rather than just listing them. Only by doing this is it possible to demonstrate the evaluative skill. You will then have a conclusion that has been justified by the evidence and argument.

It is important to use technical language when and where appropriate. Indeed the questions cited above all contain some technical word. Question 1 demands a discussion of 'proof', whilst Question 2 differentiates between the 'form' of an argument, its 'content' and its 'conclusions'. Question 3 refers to 'coherent explanation'. What has to be true about an explanation if it is claiming to be coherent?

5 The existence of God – 3

1 The Teleological Argument

> **KEY ISSUE** The Cosmological Argument attempted to infer the existence of God from the existence of the cosmos. What it really did was to look at a feature of the universe, namely that the universe cannot account for its own existence. The Teleological Argument is similar in approach. Probably the most popular and most often expressed by people, it infers the existence of God from a particular aspect or character of the world, namely the presence of order, regularity and purpose. Order, regularity and purpose are seen as marks of design, and the argument concludes that God must be the source of that design. The kind of thing that is usually appealed to as evidence of order in the universe is the solar system, with the planets revolving in their predictable orbits, or the human eye.

The word **teleological** is derived from the Greek word *telos* meaning 'end' or 'purpose'. Thus nature is viewed as directed in order that something beneficial may result. More popularly it is referred to as the 'argument from design', but this wording assumes the very thing that has to be proved. A better description would be the 'argument for design'.

Design arguments are *a posteriori* and there are various types of argument, with different philosophers giving them different names. Swinburne identifies the argument from design *and* the argument to design (also known as the **Anthropic Argument**). The former is the popular form usually involving **analogy**. The latter involves arguing that nature provides for the needs of intelligent beings. This provision requires an intelligence – God.

a) The Argument from Design

This argument has been used down the ages. For instance, Plato suggested that mind ordered all things. Nevertheless certain philosophers are particularly associated with the argument.

i) St Thomas Aquinas (1225–1274)

Aquinas (see page 26) features this argument as the fifth of his Five Ways. The heart of this argument is that non-intelligent material things produce beneficial order, and therefore require an intelligent being to bring this about, i.e. God.

ii) David Hume (1711–1776)

One of the classical statements of the argument, and one that particularly reflects eighteenth-century thinking, appears in Hume's *Dialogues concerning Natural Religion*. His book was written in the form of a dialogue between three main characters. Hence, two characters express the argument for design and then Hume, through another character (Philo), criticises the argument. This criticism is thought to be Hume's real view. However he does give a fair presentation of the case for design:

> Look round the world: Contemplate the whole and every part of it: You will find it to be nothing but one great machine, subdivided into an infinite number of lesser machines... All these various machines, and even their most minute parts are adjusted to one another with an accuracy, which ravishes into administration all men, who have ever contemplated them. The curious adapting of means to ends, throughout all nature, resembles exactly, though it much exceeds, the productions of human contrivance; of human design, thought, wisdom, and intelligence. Since therefore the effects resemble each other we are led to infer, by the rules of analogy, that the causes also resemble; and that the Author of nature is somewhat similar to the mind of man; though possessed of much larger faculties, proportional to the grandeur of the work, which he has executed. By this argument *a posteriori*, we do prove at once the existence of a Deity, and his similarity to human mind and intelligence.
>
> *Dialogues concerning Natural Religion* (1970), p. 22, ed. Wilson Pike,
> Bobbs-Merrill Educational Publishing, Indiana Press

This appeal to analogy was the popular form of expressing the argument. It was based on the argument that similar effects imply similar causes. What counted as marks of design are those features in which natural objects resemble machines made by men: the fitting of parts and what can be seen as the adaptation of means to ends. Three kinds of these features particularly impressed eighteenth-century thinkers: the world as a whole, especially the solar system as described by Newton's gravitational theory; the bodies of all sorts of plants and animals, especially certain organs like the eye; and the providential arrangement of things on the Earth.

One of the man-made objects which impressed people at that time was the pocket watch, which had just been invented. In his *Dialogue 5,* Hume uses the analogy of houses and watches, because they are so clearly produced by human designers. He says the world is like a house or a watch or a collection of houses or watches, therefore it is probably produced by something like a human designer. As has been noted, the purpose of his writing was in fact to criticise the argument, and to these criticisms we shall return later.

iii) William Paley (1743–1805)

Hume's *Dialogues* was actually published in 1779, after Hume had died. William Paley wrote his book *Natural Theology* in 1802 and, though he never refers to Hume, it is thought that he included an attempt at answering the criticisms that Hume had made of the design argument. He particularly uses the analogy of the watch (for which he is particularly remembered, though, as we have seen, it is by no means original). Suppose you are crossing a heath and come across a watch. Paley argued that even if you had never seen a watch before, you would know that this instrument did not happen by chance, but must be the result of the work of an intelligent mind. The watch demands a watchmaker. Likewise, the order in the universe demands a designer. Paley is often depicted as someone who was trying to prove God to the unbeliever. However, in the conclusion to his book he implies that he is more concerned with making things clearer to those who believe in God already.

(iv) Richard Swinburne (1934–)

Swinburne acknowledges that the argument from spatial order, used by Paley and Hume, is not very persuasive. By spatial order, Swinburne means the complex structures of things such as plants and animals. In *The Existence of God* (1979), he refers to 'the subtle and coherent arrangement of their millions of parts' (p. 134) and calls this spatial order 'the regularities of co-presence'. It is not persuasive, because such ordered complexities can be explained by modern science (theory of natural selection) and so does not require the introduction of a God.

However, Swinburne focuses on temporal order (what he calls regularities of succession). By temporal order he means the laws of nature throughout the universe. The universe is orderly, yet it could have been chaotic. Nature seems to conform to a formula. If there is an explanation to account for this, then it cannot be a scientific one because we explain the operation of scientific laws in terms of more general scientific laws. Swinburne concludes:

So either the orderliness of nature is where all explanation stops, or we must postulate an agent of great power and knowledge ... the simplest such agent is ... God. (pp. 140–141)

v) Philosophical ways to express the argument

This argument could be formally stated in a variety of ways. C Stephen Evans in *Thinking about Faith* (1985) suggests one that centres on the analogy aspect:

● Objects in nature are analogous to man-made machines.
● Man-made machines are the result of intelligent design.
● Analogous effects will have analogous causes.

Therefore, objects in nature are the result of something analogous to intelligent design.

The Argument from Design really consists of two steps:

● Showing that the world exhibits 'apparent design' (the characteristics of order, regularity, effectiveness, purpose, benefit, for example).
● The inference from this apparent design, by analogy, is of an intelligent cause.

b) The Argument from Design

This is also referred to as the **Anthropic Argument** or the argument from providence or the argument from beauty. It argues that nature seems to plan in advance for the needs of animals and humans. This planning cannot be accounted for by physical laws alone since there are innumerable ways that electrons could run. There must be more than physical laws to account for the improbability of life. It suggests mind or intelligence. Like the form of the argument by analogy, it lends itself more to an inductive formulation than to a deductive one.

Some modern proponents have argued that modern developments in science, rather than weakening the teleological argument, have lent support to it. Appeal is made to the intricate relationships found in biochemistry relating to the development of living organisms, and evolution, suggesting that this could not have occurred by accident, but rather required some overall direction. It looks like things have worked together to our benefit, almost as if the universe in some sense had known that we were coming. S Davis (*God, Reason and Theistic Proofs*, 1997) lists a number of examples that seem to be fine-tuned for life. Included in his examples (pp. 108—111) are:

● **Cosmological constants**: These are items like the gravitational constant, the speed of light, the basic properties of elementary particles, and Planck's constant. All these constants could have been different, yet their values all fall within a very narrow range that makes life possible.

● **The Rate of expansion of the Big Bang**: This focuses on the speed at which bits of matter flew apart from other bits of matter soon after the Big Bang. Galaxies would have been impossible had the expansion rate and total mass of universe not been finely tuned to each other.
● **Thermal properties of water**: If the earth were either 5% closer or 1% further from the sun, life would not be possible. The earth has an atmosphere, which protects it from ultra radiation; and oceans serve as a thermostat shielding us from extreme temperatures.

Similar arguments speak in terms of 'probability', concluding that the order of the universe is statistically speaking 'beyond chance'. Often terms such as 'an anti-chance factor' are introduced. In 1985, the then Bishop of Birmingham, Hugh Montifiore, wrote a book called *The Probability of God*. This argued that, given the findings of science, the most reasonable explanation for the character of the universe is God.

In a similar vein, F R Tennant (*Philosophical Theology*, 1930) argues that the universe is not just beautiful in places; it is saturated with beauty from the microscopic to the macroscopic level. Likewise Swinburne argues in terms of probabilities and God being the simplest explanation to account for the universe.

c) An initial difficulty

Before dealing in detail with Hume's criticisms, it is worth noting a general point of confusion about the analogy approach. It is by no means clear in the analogy whether the machine, etc. is being compared to:

(i) the whole of the universe or
(ii) parts of the universe.

If it is (i) then how can you say that the whole of the universe is working to an end or purpose? It certainly is not obvious. Many argue that to conclude such a thing requires knowledge obtainable only from being outside the universe (although it could be obtained by revelation).
Alternatively, in (ii) it may be possible to show that parts of the universe work to an end or purpose, *but* it is a fallacy of logic to then argue from that, that the whole works to a particular end or purpose.

d) Hume's criticisms

Hume worked on his critique of the argument of design for some 25 years, culminating in his now famous book *Dialogues concerning Natural Religion*. Some of his friends urged him to abandon it or even destroy it, regarding it as too dangerous and irreligious. However, he made plans for it to be published after his death. His criticisms of the argument cover several points.

i) An unsound analogy

The strength of the argument depends upon the similarity between the things held to be analogous (i.e. the machine and the world). The greater the similarity, the stronger is the argument; the weaker the similarity, the weaker is the argument. But, said Hume, the two analogies are far apart. Our world is *not* like a machine at all since it is composed of vegetables and animals. It is more organic than it is mechanical.

Neither is it philosophically sound to argue that intelligence is the necessary governing principle behind the world. Hume pointed out that there were lots of alternative governing principles (generation, vegetation, gravity). Why should one of these not be the dominant principle? Indeed, why should different principles not rule over their own natural domains: vegetation in plants, generation in animals, gravity in movements of planets? We cannot project from one limited area to another part or to the whole of nature.

Hume re-emphasised the point that the world did *not* closely resemble something man-made by referring to a house; if we see a house we conclude with certainty that it had an architect or builder because we have seen it being built – *but* the universe does not bear such a resemblance that with certainty we could infer a similar cause (i.e. intelligence, thought). Also a number of people are involved in designing a house so perhaps, by analogy, there are a team of gods who designed the world.

ii) Similar effects do not necessarily imply similar causes

Following on from the above points about the lack of similarities between a machine and the world, Hume goes further by questioning whether it is a sound notion that similar effects result necessarily from similar causes. To know that an orderly universe must arise from intelligence and thought, we would have to have experienced the origin of the world. Why should not similar effects be the result of *different* causes?

iii) Other possible analogies

This has already been hinted at in (i) above. Hume argued that 'the world plainly resembles more an animal or a vegetable than it does a watch or a knitting loom'. In particular he argued that the world could be compared to a carrot. The relevance of this is that if the analogy is made with the carrot then the mark of design in the world could be caused by something similar to generation or vegetation. The natural world may possess some inner self-regulation and growth. Had Hume lived long enough he may well have quoted **Darwinism** as a possible example. This sees beneficial adaptations explained in non-personal terms by means of natural selection.

Indeed, Hume argued that at its base, intelligence is itself caused by the process of generation! Surely the process of causes continues since intelligence requires a cause. Hence you end up with an infinite regression of causes.

iv) Analogy makes God more human than divine

The more you press the analogy of the man-made machine (e.g. watch) with the universe, the more human you have to make God (similar effects implies similar causes). For instance:

- Infinity could not be attributed to any of the attributes of God. For, as the cause ought only to be proportional to the effect, and the effect is not infinite, so neither have we any reason to ascribe infinity to God.
- Likewise perfection cannot be ascribed. It is impossible for us to tell whether this system contains any great faults. Even if it were perfect, it would remain uncertain whether all the excellences can be ascribed to the workmen. For instance, many worlds might have been botched and bungled before this system was made.
- Hume drove his point home by suggesting the following:

  This world is very faulty and imperfect, and was only the first rude essay of some infant deity who afterwards abandoned it, ashamed of his lame performance; it is the work only of some inferior deity and is the object of derision to his superiors; it is the production of old age in some superannuated deity, and ever since his death has run on from the first impulse and active force which he gave it …

v) Analogy leads to a non-moral God

Hume listed some unpleasant features of nature, e.g. earthquakes, war, disease, and questioned how the planning and design could be that of a just and good God. Workmen have to be judged in proportion to the quality of the work produced! Equally Hume argued that you cannot attribute to the cause anything more than is sufficient to produce the effect. He claimed that a more plausible hypothesis was that of a God who had no moral character. Alternatively there could be two forces, one good and one evil.

vi) Other explanations for apparent order

Hume suggested that we cannot be sure that the so-called organised universe is not the result of some blind, cosmic accident. Indeed any universe is bound to have the appearance of design. There could be no universe at all if the parts of it were not mutually adapted to some degree.

e) Further arguments

Other arguments against the Teleological Argument include the following.

● Darwinism, with its appeal for explanation in natural selection, dealt a severe blow to the Teleological Argument.
● The debate begins with 'this world' and concludes with concepts of which we have no experience, e.g. infinite, uncaused.
● A recent development in linguistic philosophy (see page 119) has centred on the issue of whether statements are meaningful. One conclusion is that a meaningful statement is one where we know what would disprove it. Hence A J Ayer argued that:

the world is designed is a meaningless statement (since) until we can say what the world would have to be like, to be not designed, we cannot conclude that the world is designed.

In a similar way, it could be argued that any world, whatever its form, will appear consistent with the idea of a designed universe.

● It has been argued that there is no need to think of things in the universe operating in the light of any kind of purpose. Rather they can be said to come about not in order that something may be achieved, but only as a result of what has already occurred.
● Unless the universe was an orderly place, people would not be around to comment on the fact. Hence there is nothing surprising in the fact that people find order. They couldn't find anything else. Swinburne has responded to this criticism by using his illustration of the card-shuffling machine (*The Existence of God*, p. 138). He comments:

The teleologist's starting point is not that we perceive order rather than disorder, but that order rather than disorder is there. Maybe only if order is there can we know what is there, but that makes what is there no less extraordinary and in need of explanation.

● We have no certain reason to believe that the universe will continue to behave in an orderly way.

f) Conclusions

Most scholars concede that Hume made some valid points against the argument from design, and in particular about the analogy approach. Certainly in its deductive form it fails, but many find it persuasive as an inductive argument. Kant, though regarding the argument as invalid, stated 'This proof always deserves to be mentioned with respect. It is the most accordant with the common reason of mankind.' (*Critique of Pure Reason*, 1781).

Despite the general acceptance of some form of the evolutionary theory, many feel it does not eliminate God. This is because the old notion of external design has been replaced by inner self-regulation; and this, in turn, is seen as God's design. In other words, evolution is seen as the means by which God achieves his purpose. In a similar way some argue that evolution is guided by God at key stages, so making sure it reaches the desired end. Supporters of these views are known as 'theistic evolutionists', seeing no contradiction between God as designer and evolution. Still others argue that evolution is not proven and that God remains the designer of the universe.

Appeals to recent scientific findings have, for some, drawn attention to the complexities of nature and led them to conclude that the most *reasonable* explanation is God, whilst for others (e.g. Richard Dawkins and Peter Atkins), it has revealed that random changes can lead to order and complex systems can be self-arranging. The debate seems not to have lost any of its vigour:

> ... far from being the 'terminus' of the quest for intelligibility and explanation in the universe, God is the terminal illness of reason.
>
> (Peter Atkins in an article in *Dialogue*, Issue 10 April 1998).

Answering questions on Chapter 5

It should be remembered that the Teleological Argument has two forms: (i) *from* design and (ii) *to* design.

Questions will usually ask you to state the argument so it is important to explain the analogy. Both man-made machines (such as the watch) and the universe are said to share common features: namely order, regularity, purpose and benefit. Since the man-made machine has an intelligent designer, so by analogy, the universe also has an intelligent designer, called God. Similar effects imply similar causes.

As regards the argument *to* design (anthropic), there are some good examples from science showing how complex and intricate the universe is, and thereby rejecting chance as the explanation. In particular see *Philosophy of Religion: Selected Readings* (ed. Michael Peterson) pp. 198–210.

Once again the critiques need to be debated rather than just listed, if evaluation skills are going to be shown. Consider the following question:

1. 'Design, and the working out of an underlying purpose, is evident in the world.' The only reasonable explanation for this is that there is a designer, and that the designer is God.' **a)** 'Design and the working out of an underlying purpose is evident in the world.' What is the evidence on which this claim is based? **b)** Assess the claim that 'The only reasonable explanation for this is that there is a designer.' **c)** Comment on the conclusion that 'the designer is God.'

Note that in part a) the argument is not asked for. What are required are examples of order and regularity and also evidence of an underlying purpose such as the anthropic principle. In part b) the criticisms would be looked for, such as those of Hume. However, these must be argued in the light of the stimulus quote, namely posing some alternative explanations (evolution), questioning a single designer, challenging that the designer still exists and finally debating what constitutes a reasonable explanation. How reasonable is God as an explanation? Who designed the designer?

In part c) such questions as whether the traditional God is the designer can be challenged. What about evil? Is God the designer and creator?

6 The existence of God – 4

1 The Moral Argument

KEY ISSUE This argument seeks to show that in the existence of God we find the best solution to the common human experience of **moral** consciousness and obligation.

As with all the theistic proofs, there are various forms of the Moral Argument. They fall into four approaches:

- Aquinas and the Fourth of his Five Ways.
- Our conscience and sense of obligation only make sense if there is a divine lawgiver who has sovereign claims.
- If there is no God, there seems no reason to be moral.
- God is required for morality to achieve its end, according to Kant.

a) Aquinas

Some people have used Aquinas' Fourth Way as an entry to the Moral Argument, though Aquinas does not specifically refer to morality as such but rather true, noble and good.

He said that we experience things in the world which are noble, true, good and valuable. These things must take their reality from things which are more true, noble, good and valuable. To avoid an infinite regression, there must be something which is the most true, noble, good and valuable. This is what we call 'God'.

By 'noble' he seems to mean the quality whereby something is valuable in itself rather than as a means to some other good thing. The argument tries to show that there is something which is the cause in every being of its goodness and every other possible perfection. It is a mixture of Platonic and Aristotelian ideas, which understood each substance to be a self-contained teleological (goal-orientated) system. The goal to which all things are striving must actually exist. That pure actuality is what we call God.

b) The nature of moral experience

There seem to be a number of human experiences concerning moral consciousness and moral obligation that require explanation. For many, the only satisfactory explanation is the existence of a God.

- There seems to be a universal experience that there *is* a right and wrong. Certainly all cultures do not agree about *what* is right and wrong but they all appeal to some moral authority which is more than just pragmatism.
- Rightness and wrongness have meaning independently of our judgement of them. That is, they seem to be objective values and do not depend on what we believe or do not believe about them.
- A popular form of this approach sees conscience as the voice of the lawgiver (God). John Newman wrote:

  If, as is the case, we feel responsibility, are ashamed, are frightened, at transgressing the voice of conscience, this implies that there is One to whom we are responsible, before whom we are ashamed, whose claim upon us we fear.

  Grammar of Assent (1870) p. 83

  Obedience and guilt are only seen to be meaningful if there is a person to whom responsibility is due.
- In a similar way, it is argued that laws imply a lawgiver. There are objectively binding moral laws which can only be explained by the existence of a moral God. Moral claims are best explained in terms of a personal God, given the personal source of ordinary claims and commands. Once we perceive something to be right, we can no longer view it neutrally. There is a pressure on us to respond.

The main criticism to this approach questions the assumption that there are objectively binding moral laws. In other words, our sense of conscience and obligation could be accounted for *without* appealing to the existence of God. Alternative possible explanations include the following.

- **Cultural relativism**: Every society approves and disapproves of particular actions, and teaches its young to think of such actions as 'right' or 'wrong'. Which acts are designated right or wrong differs from one culture to another. Thus morality is a product of human culture. The reason we feel guilt, etc. lies in 'socialisation' (e.g. values taught to us when we were children).

- **Emotivism:** When a person states that an act is wrong they are not stating a fact, but merely expressing their own emotion or attitude about the act, i.e. something is 'good' if I approve of it and 'bad' if I do not.
- **Evolution:** Human beings who had the notion to be kind, helpful, etc. were more likely to survive in the process of natural selection. This characteristic then became genetically transmitted.

This form of the Moral Argument rests on the assumption that no adequate account can be given for a person's sense of moral obligation. It is certainly contestable whether this assumption is true. For example, unjust societies are a threat to their members, who have good reason to be just if they want to survive and enjoy the many benefits that we know to be possible only in a just society. Hence God's existence is no longer necessary as the source of authority and ultimate sanction.

Even if the moral law requires a source of authority and sanction, that does not mean that there is a source or sanction. What I require to be the case hardly brings the case into reality!

c) If God does not exist, 'anything goes'

To deny that God exists is to deny the source of authority for good moral behaviour and to deny the ultimate sanction against evil behaviour. Therefore, there would be no reason to behave in a good way. Hence there would be no reason not to act according to our own whims. John Hick points out that on humanist presuppositions, it would be inconsistent to praise self-sacrifice for the sake of the human community since 'it is unreasonable for anything to be of

Figure 2 - Immanuel Kant

more value to a man than his own existence' (*Arguments for the Existence of God*, 1970). In other words, it becomes very difficult to *justify* such heroic acts if God does not exist.

d) Kant's arguments (God is required for morality to achieve its end)

Kant's moral argument is an example of what he means by the postulate of practical reason. He wants to show that God's existence is implied by man's moral experience.

To understand the argument, one has to understand something about the thinking of Kant. He argued that the mind determines the way in which we experience things, rather than the external things in themselves. All we know comes from sense experiences organised by our minds. We cannot know 'things in themselves', but only things as we perceive them to be.

Kant held that the 'categories' by which we understand the world – categories like space, time, and causality – were *not* derived from experience. Rather the mind imposes categories on all its experiences (e.g. we cannot prove anything has a cause; we assume it and confirm by experience).

Thus Kant argued that we cannot prove that we ought to do something by analysing it, since we will never have enough evidence. For Kant, the idea of moral obligation comes from within ourselves – and we experience it as the '**categorical imperative**'.

Being moral was a case of following this categorical imperative. A genuinely moral action would be one that was done on the maxim which we could will to be a universal law. Thus an immoral action would be one whose underlying maxim could not be intelligibly willed to be universal law (e.g. lying to suit my own ends would not be wise for a universal law).

This is the test for good and bad actions. Reason, not feelings, is the guide, and good acts are obligatory because they are rational.

(i) The moral argument for the existence of God
The argument for God can be presented by the following steps:

● Our moral experience shows that we are under an obligation to achieve goodness or virtue, and not merely an 'average' level of morality but the highest standard possible. (We recognise an obligation to achieve what is best–real virtue.)
● But not only this, we recognise also that true virtue should be rewarded by happiness, for it would not be a rationally satisfying state of affairs if happiness came to the unvirtuous or unhappiness to the virtuous. If people were virtuous but were also in pain and misery, their

virtue would still be valuable but nevertheless, the total situation would not be the best possible.
- The desired state of affairs in which man is both virtuous and happy is called by Kant the 'summum bonum' (highest good). This we recognise to be what ought to happen.
- Now, in Kant's famous argument, 'ought' implies 'can', i.e. an obligation to achieve something implies the possibility that the goal can be achieved (otherwise there can be no obligation). It has to be possible, therefore, for the summum bonum to be achieved.
- However, while humans can achieve virtue, it is clearly outside their power to ensure that virtue is rewarded or coincides with happiness.
- Thus there is a need to postulate the existence of God as the one who has the power to bring virtue and happiness into harmony. Such proportioning clearly does not take place before death, so Kant also argued that there must be survival after death.

Note that Kant was not arguing that morality is invalid if God's existence is denied. For Kant, the fact that it is a duty or obligation is sufficient reason to do it. However, he thought that God was demanded if the goal of morality was to be realised.

(ii) Criticisms
Criticisms include such points as:

- Kant argued that 'ought implies can'. If he meant that it was logically possible to bring about the summum bonum, then all he was saying was that it was not a logical contradiction. But just because it is not a logical contradiction does not therefore mean that it factually happens. If he meant that it factually happens, we can ask the questions 'Why must it? How can anyone know?' In other words, we question his assumption.
- Why make the assumption that only God can bring about the highest good? 'Why not a pantheon of angels?' suggests Brian Davies (An Introduction to the Philosophy of Religion, 1982, p. 96).
- Why make the assumption that virtue must be rewarded with happiness?
- Sense of duty can be explained by other means, e.g. socialisation.

e) Conclusions

Therefore, though the arguments fail, they do highlight the point that the rational moral agent 'must believe that a moral reality lies behind the natural order' (C Stephen Evans, *Thinking about Faith*, 1985). In a similar way, Stephen T Davis sees the key issue as to whether 'it is possible to give a compelling account of morality in purely naturalistic terms' (*God, Reason and Theistic Proofs*, 1997).

Answering questions on Chapter 6

The Moral Argument is one that many students find difficult. Essentially it falls into three main areas: moral consciousness, moral obligation and Kant's *summum bonum*. The arguments against are attempts to account for the experience of morality without the need of a God, in particular the dilemma as to whether objectively binding morals can exist without a God.

One useful approach when considering arguments is to state what you regard as the strongest argument *against* your own personal view and examine how you would reply to it. This develops the ability to appreciate the opposing views of an argument.

Another activity might be to consider whether anyone who was rational could sacrifice their own life in saving someone from being burnt alive in a house fire, unless they believed in the existence of God.

It should be noted that Kant did not argue that there were no morals without God, rather that God was required to guarantee the *summum bonum*. Much of the argument is based around the claim that there are objective moral laws. The criticisms challenge that fact and ask not only whether morals are objective but also, even if they were, if God is the only way they could be objective?

A possible question could be:

1. 'The moral argument does not prove that God exists, but it does make it probable that God exists.' Discuss this assertion.

This question allows not just for a rehearsal of the Moral Argument but the issue of proof. Is proof deductive only? What of the inductive argument? What of the cumulative argument for the existence of God? What of degrees of probability?

7 The existence of God – 5

1 The Religious Experience Argument

KEY ISSUE It is an undisputed fact that people claim to have experiences of God or experiences which are in some way revelatory (reveal something of God to them). The argument from experience to prove the existence of God rests on the view that belief in God is reasonable, not because its truth is entailed by a series of premises, but because God can be somehow directly encountered or immediately perceived. It is further argued that experience of God is a reason for believing in Him even for people who lack belief.

There are a number of ways of expressing the argument, for example:

- If someone experiences an entity, then the entity exists.
- Some people have experienced God.

Therefore God exists.

a) Differences between 'religious' and 'ordinary' experiences

In 1969, Sir Alister Hardy set up the Religious Experience Research Unit (RERU) in Oxford, with the object of examining the extent and nature of the religious experiences of people in Britain. Part of this research was published by David Hay (*Inner Space*, 1987) and revealed that 25-45% of the population of Britain had been aware of a presence or power beyond themselves.

From questionnaires and interviews, the responses about religious experience indicate that:

the experience has always been quite different from any other type of experience they have ever had … and usually induces in the person concerned a conviction that the everyday world is not the whole of reality; there is another dimension to life … awareness of its presence affects the person's view of the world, it alters behaviour and changes attitudes.

Inner Space

Among the differences between 'religious' and 'ordinary' experiences are:

- Religious experiences are wholly other from what is customary and usual. God is experienced, as opposed to everyday physical objects. There is a spiritual change that clearly has a religious dimension.
- It is not usual to be able to describe the religious experience.
- The religious experience is not universal to human beings (i.e. we do not all have religious experiences but we all experience a tree, etc.).
- Human beings basically use the same conceptual scheme when they describe an ordinary experience. Regardless of culture we all describe a tree in the same way. However with religious experience, though the feeling may be similar (e.g. awe), the object is different (e.g. Jesus, Krishna). In other words, religious experiences have different interpretations in different cultures.
- Often a religious experience is a **subjective** experience, whereas an ordinary experience is **objective**.
- Religious experience cannot generally be checked, whereas an ordinary experience is open to checking (e.g. can be seen by others).
- It gives insight into the unseen whereas the ordinary gives no insight into other realms.
- You cannot experience God unless He allows you to. In contrast, an ordinary experience may be experienced by anyone in the right place at the right time with the requisite sense organs.

b) Types of religious experience

Religious experiences have been described across religions and through the centuries. Some are spontaneous whilst others are the result of training and discipline, but they all share the common feature of an awareness of the divine. This awareness can take the form of:

- A sense of oneness or union with the divine.
- A sense of dependence on the divine.
- A sense of separateness from the divine.

Clearly any experience may contain more than one of these elements.

A definition of 'religious experience' could be 'an experience that has religious insight'. This insight is usually into the unseen dimensions of existence and may well affect the outlook and behaviour of the recipient of the experience. They realise that the everyday world is not the whole of reality.

Recently, Swinburne (*The Existence of God*, 1979) has centred on religious experience as a key argument for God's existence. He identifies five types of religious experience in which a person seems to perceive God:

- In perceiving a perfectly normal non-religious object, e.g. a night sky.
- In perceiving a very unusual public object, e.g. the resurrection appearances of Jesus.

These first two are both public events. The last three are private:

- In having private sensations that are describable using normal vocabulary, e.g. Joseph's dream of the angel.
- In having private sensations that are not describable using normal vocabulary, e.g. a **mysticism** (see below).
- Having no sensations. The person would be unable to refer to anything in particular that made it seem they were experiencing God. 'It just did!'

i) Mysticism

A mystical experience is the name given to the experience of having apprehended an ultimate reality that is difficult to express using normal vocabulary. It characteristically involves some kind of sense of the unity of all things in one substance and one life. There are numerous ways of classifying the experiences. For instance, Stace (*Mysticism and Philosophy*, Macmillan, 1960) distinguished between an *extrovertive* (outward-looking) and an *introvertive* (inward-looking) mystical experience. Jonathan Webber (*Revelation and Religious Experience*, 1995) summarises the difference between the extrovertive and introvertive as follows:

> The extrovertive is one where the plurality of objects in the world are transfigured into a single living entity. In contrast, the introvertive mystic speaks of losing their identity as a separate individual and slowly merging into the divine unity.

He gives an example of an introvertive mystic experience which comes from the Chandogya Upanishads:

> As rivers flow to their rest in the ocean and there leave behind them name and form, so the knower, liberated from name and form, reaches that divine Person beyond the beyond.

Others distinguish between 'theistic mysticism' and 'monistic mysticism'. The latter involves an awareness of the soul, selfhood or consciousness rather than God. However, the classic account of mysticism is given by William James (*The Varieties of Religious Experience*, 1902) who lists with examples four main characteristics of mystic experiences:

- *Ineffability*: They are states of feeling so unlike anything else that it is not possible to import or transfer them to others. They defy expression. Descriptions such as 'the dissolution of the personal ego' and 'the sense of peace and sacredness' are empty phrases to those who have not experienced such things.
- *Noetic quality*: Though ineffable, the mystic experience produces states of insight into truths unobtainable by the intellect alone. They are revelations. They are not trivial. They are universal and eternal truths.
- *Transiency*: The religious experience does not last for long, usually half an hour or so. Though they are remembered, they are imperfectly recalled, but recognised if they recur. If a series of mystic experiences take place, then usually there is some sort of development of inner richness. They usually leave the recipient with a profound sense of the importance of the experience.
- *Passivity*: Mystical states can be helped by such things as 'fixing the attention' or 'going through certain bodily movements', but when the state occurs, the mystic feels as if they are taken over by a superior power. This can result in phenomena that suggests alternative personality states – e.g. prophetic speech, speaking in tongues.

One of the classic mystics connected to Christian tradition is St Teresa of Avila (1515–1582). In her writings the ineffable characteristic is prevalent, e.g. in *The Collected Work of St Teresa of Avila* (ICS Publications, 1987):

> the soul is fully awake as regards God, but wholly asleep as regards things of this world.

> God establishes himself in the interior of this soul in such a way that when I return to myself, it is wholly impossible for me to doubt that I have been in God, and God in me.

Associated with Teresa's 'raptures' are always visions. Her most famous vision involved her seeing a small angel with a beautiful face holding 'a long golden spear', tipped with a 'little fire', which he thrust into her heart. She says:

> … it penetrated into my entrails. When he drew out the spear he seemed to be drawing them out with it, leaving me all on fire with a wondrous love for God.

William James gives a list of examples that range from those that have no special religious significance (e.g. 'I've heard that said all my life, but never realised its full meaning until now') to those that are intensely religious.

Most mystical experiences occur when in a conscious state and the person differentiates between that experience and a dream. William James reports the following example:

> There came upon me a sense of immense exultation and joyousness followed by an intellectual illumination impossible to describe. Among other things, I did not merely come to believe, but I saw that the universe is not composed of dead matter but rather a living Presence; I became conscious in myself of eternal life … The vision lasted a few seconds and was gone but the memory of it and the sense of reality of what it taught have remained … I knew that what the vision showed me was true.

Another approach to analysing some mystical experiences is by reference to the Numinous. This term is often used to describe the experience in which God's separateness is highlighted. It was coined by Rudolf Otto (1869-1937) in his book *The Idea of the Holy* (1917). The word comes from the Latin *numen* meaning divinity.

For Otto, religion sprang from experience of the holy. However because this word had so many associations, he used *numen*. It is something that is 'wholly other' than the natural world. He analysed this type of experience in terms of the Latin phrase *mysterium tremendum et fascinans*. Ninian Smart explains this as 'a mystery which is awe-inspiring and fascinating and points towards the Transcendent'. People are drawn towards it, hoping for holiness yet also realising that there is but One Being who is holy.

In his book, Otto illustrates this type of experience by examples from a variety of religions. This emphasis on the 'otherness' of God tends to put an impersonal idea at the heart of religion.

In contrast Martin Buber (1878–1965) stresses personal relationships and that which underlies them. In his book *I and Thou* (1937) Buber argues for two kinds of relationships: The I–It and the I–Thou. The former is when we view people and things as merely phenomena. By probing deeper we can enter the second relationship both with people and things, such that we can call it a personal relationship.

> It is here that we encounter a Thou over against our I. And this is the realm also where we encounter God.

This approach is interpreted as an experience of God through our relationships with people and the world.

ii) Conversion

Conversion denotes the changing from one set of beliefs to another. In religious terms a person can convert from one faith to another: from being an atheist to being a theist; from being a believer to being a non-believer.

Conversion can be a sudden process or a gradual one. Often it involves feelings of guilt (a conviction of 'sin'), a search for faith, sometimes voices but usually at least some sort of divine communication, and a resulting assurance or feeling of certainty.

Possibly the best known example is that of Saul (later called St Paul) who had a conversion experience on his way to Damascus, where he had intended to persecute some Christians (see Acts 9:1–18). Paul's conversion was not putting on a patch of holiness *but* rather it was holiness woven into all his power, principles and practice. He described himself as a new man, a new creation.

Another well-known example is that of John Wesley. He was aware that he did not have the faith in Christ as a personal saviour that he saw others had. However, on 24 May 1738, at a meeting of an evangelical society in Aldersgate, London he had a conversion experience. He wrote in his Journal for that day:

> I felt my heart strangely warmed. I felt I did trust in Christ, Christ alone, for salvation; and an assurance was given me, that He had taken away my sins, even mine …

The examples of gradual conversion usually involve the building up, piece by piece, of a new set of beliefs and habits. However, even this type of conversion often has critical points at which the movement forward seems much more rapid. One of the characteristics of this gradual conversion is a voluntary and conscious act by the person.

William James concludes by noting that the persons who have passed through conversion, having once taken a stand for the religious life, tend to feel themselves identified with it, no matter how much their religious enthusiasm declines.

iii) Prayer

The wide sense of the word **prayer** includes every kind of inward communion or conversation with the power recognised as divine. This includes adoration of God (praising God), confession, thanksgiving and petition (asking). Prayer in this wide sense is the very essence of religion. Indeed, it is prayer that distinguishes the religious phenomenon from other phenomena such as the purely moral. Prayer is the conviction that something is genuinely transacted; that things that cannot be realised in any other way come about.

William James uses the example of George Muller of Bristol, who died in 1898. He was well known for running orphanages and schools and lived by prayer, believing that God provides. His custom was never to run up bills, not even for a week. He also made it a point never to tell people of his needs. His biography relates the vast number of times that, for instance, there was no food to feed the children in the orphanage with, and then it would be provided by someone.

Many religious people claim that through a prayerful life they experience 'coincidences' that make it seem that their life is guided.

c) Is a religious experience authentic?

As has been noted above, a religious experience cannot be authenticated in the way that an ordinary sense experience can be. Religious experiences are very much a private matter rather than a public one, and it is not possible therefore to check someone else's religious experience. If the event is a public one, then it still entails a religious interpretation. Even more problematic is the private event.

A number of points have been discussed about this whole area.

i) Is an 'experience of God' a philosophically sound notion?

When people try to describe an experience of God, they tend to make comparisons that raise problems philosophically. Analogies are appealed to, to justify the philosophical notion of a religious experience of God, but many argue that the analogies have weaknesses:

- **It is like a sense experience**: People argue that just as you can encounter a table, you can also encounter God, but the two are very different. For instance, God is not material, nor does He have a definite location. Also, claims can be checked of encounters with objects, but when the object is God, they are not verifiable.
- **It is similar to an experience of people**: People argue that just as we are known to each other by a kind of direct apprehension rather than through our physical body, so in the same way we experience God who is non-corporeal.

   Firstly this assumes that people are non-corporeal (i.e. dualistic nature). Secondly, even if people are mind and body, we still encounter them when they have bodies. Knowing they are there involves knowing that their bodies exist. In contrast, God has no body at all. Therefore an encounter with God is radically different from an encounter with a person. Thirdly, we are aware of how many people we are having an encounter with (i.e. they are physical units distinguishable in some way from others), because it involves reference to material factors. However, when we encounter God, He is not material, yet is said to be one being. Finally, there are theological reasons to question the idea that God can be known in the same way as we can know a person. According to the Bible, God is not a person, e.g. 'God is Love'.
- **Can God be recognised?**: The problem arises as to how you can distinguish God from other possible objects of experience. For instance, God is said to be the Creator. How would you recognise that attribute? God is said also to be omnipresent, infinite, omnipotent and eternal. But how, simply by virtue of an awareness of an object of experience, can anything be recognised to be that? To recognise omniscience, you would have to be omniscient yourself!

   One solution is to argue that an experience of God would be a self-authenticating experience. But feelings of certainty can occur when in fact I am wrong. Just declaring that 'You know' is insufficient. There must be reasons as well as convictions.

● **Direct experience of God is impossible**: Some claim that the finite cannot experience the infinite – so we cannot experience God. Others argue that to speak of a direct experience is not philosophically correct since we infer and interpret every experience. For instance, even an ordinary object is mediated and interpreted via our sense data and organs.

Indeed, it could be argued that the religious person interprets experience according to a religious framework of life, whilst the atheist interprets it as purely natural events. Hick referred to this as 'experiencing-as' and illustrated it using the ambiguous figure of the 'rabbit-duck'.

ii) Is there is a natural explanation?

When we speak of an experience there are two distinct elements: that which is experienced (**objective**) and my experience of what is experienced (**subjective**). Many people question the objective, claiming that there is no religious reality, only the person's wrong interpretation of the source of the experience. Hence various other sources are offered and the following points made.

● **Experience is often deceptive**: e.g. hallucinations. However, mistakes do not demand that all experiences are therefore in error. It is true that we may regard a particular witness as unreliable, but for the argument to be valid, all people who claim experience would have to be known to be unreliable. Clearly such a position is difficult to maintain.

● **The psychological**: For instance, conversion may meet the psychological needs of people. Freud saw religious experience as a reaction to a hostile world. We feel helpless and seek a father figure, thus we create a God who is able to satisfy our needs. Jung suggested the archetype deep within us. Sexual frustration is said to be the explanation of St Teresa of Avilas's mystic experiences, especially the one involving the spear! Appeal is made to recent research that includes the link between certain personality types and religious interest, as well as talk of identifying 'a religious gene'.

However, even if people need a father figure, it does not mean that God is not like that. There does still remain the possibility that such a state is a necessary requirement for the experience, but such a state would not necessarily negate acclaimed experience of God.

iii) Reasons that make it unlikely

Some people feel that there is an inconsistency about the argument, that if it were true then surely certain things would be expected to follow, e.g. the experience should be fairly uniform.

● **There is no God, therefore the experience of God cannot be valid**: However, this is an *a priori* conviction, whose reasons would need to be examined. This has gained strength in recent times with the debate about whether God is really an object / being. Some reject the traditional understanding of the word 'God' and see it more as 'a form of life' which the believer inhabits. It is a way of expressing a particular way of looking at the world and does not refer to any external, objective being. For further discussion on this approach see Chapter 14 on Religious Language.

● **Lack of uniformity of experience**: The fact that different experiences are recounted does not mean that they are therefore all in error. Also this explanation implies that the different experiences are logically incompatible, which is not necessarily true. The lack of uniformity may also be due to the interpretation rather than the falsity of the actual religious experience.

● **Not all experience it**: Surely if there was a God He would want everyone to know about Him and therefore all should have religious experiences. However, it could be argued that some precondition, like faith, is required. Also the initiative may have to come from God who may be selective. Alternatively perhaps He does reveal himself but we are unable to see it (like a tone-deaf person unable to appreciate music). Indeed, believers assume often that others can have the experience and even encourage them to do so (e.g. evangelism).

d) Conclusions

Religious experience is not a conclusive argument for the existence of God. One may believe that what is experienced is actually God, but there is always the possibility that others may interpret it differently.

Whether religious experience is seen to be caused by God will depend to a great extent upon individual pre-suppositions. If one's pre-suppositions favour particular types of experiences one is likely to be convinced of reports of them.

However, it is not proof because it does not compel you to conclude that God exists, but criteria may be applied that would add weight to the validity of the religious experience:

● It must be in keeping with the character of God as made known in different ways, e.g. through natural theology, agreement with doctrine, resemblance of experience to classic cases in religious tradition as judged by spiritual authorities.

● The results of the experience should make a noticeable difference to the religious life of the person. It should lead to a new life marked by virtues such as wisdom, humility and goodness of life. It should build up the community rather than destroy it. Teresa of Avila said:

Though the devil can give some pleasures – only God-produced experiences leave the soul in peace and tranquillity and devotion to God.

- The person should be regarded as someone who is mentally and psychologically well-balanced.

Wainwright (*Philosophy of Religion*, 1988) comments that the only conclusive grounds for rejecting religious experiences would be:

- Proofs of the non-existence of God and other supernatural entities.
- Good reasons for thinking that the perceptual claims immediately based on these experiences are inconsistent.
- Evidence that the experiences are produced by natural mechanisms known to systematically cause false beliefs and delusive experiences.

Wainwright's personal conclusion is that, so far, critics have not provided these grounds. For a very different conclusion read Chapter 10 in Mackie's book *The Miracle of Theism* (1992).

Recently Richard Swinburne has given much importance to the argument from religious experience (*The Existence of God*, 1979), as does Caroline Franks Davis' book *The Evidential Force of Religious Experience* (1989). In particular, Swinburne puts forward two principles.

(i) The Principle of Credulity
In the absence of special considerations, if it seems that X is present to a person, then probably X is present. In short, what one seems to perceive is probably the case. He points out that unless we assume this we cannot know anything.

However, his special considerations are:

- If subject 'S' was unreliable.
- If similar perceptions are shown to be false.
- If there is strong evidence that X did not exist.
- If X can be accounted for in other ways.

(ii) The Principle of Testimony
In the absence of special considerations, it is reasonable to believe that the experiences of others are probably as they report them.

In other words we should believe other people unless we have good reason not to. The significance of this approach is to put the onus on the sceptic to show that religious experience should be rejected, rather than for the believer to show that it is true. This is particularly important as a cumulative argument if all the other arguments for the existence of God are evenly balanced.

In conclusion, it should also be noted that some argue that the origin of an experience is irrelevant. The fact that the source may be an ordinary experience does not mean that the experience cannot become a religious one by the interpretation of the subject.

Answering questions on Chapter 7

Now try to list the differences between ordinary and religious experiences and show the information in a chart. As you will discover, some of the characteristics seem to appear in *both* sections. What might this suggest about some religious experiences? How might a religious believer account for these similarities?

It is helpful to be able to illustrate answers about religious experience with some actual examples. Some are given in the chapter but you should add to these from your own reading.

The sorts of questions asked include:

I. **a)** What are the distinctive features of a 'mystical' experience? **b)** Consider the view that calling an experience 'mystical' is doing no more than giving an ordinary experience a religious interpretation. Evaluate this claim.

In part **b)** it would be expected that you would argue the case of why it could be regarded as an ordinary experience (natural explanations). Also you would need to challenge that view and highlight not only differences but also reasons for thinking mystical experiences are authentic (see pp. 57–58). Finally you may want to draw attention to the fact that if God is in all things then in one sense every 'ordinary' experience is a religious experience.

For a 45-minute exam essay answer the average student writes about 800–1000 words. Where questions are structured it is usual to indicate how many each part is worth. This mark allocation is a guide to time allocation expected.

8 Miracles

1 What is a miracle?

> **KEY ISSUE** The debate about miracles revolves around two key questions: 'What is a miracle? and 'Is it reasonable to believe a miracle has taken place?'

The previous chapters have considered the evidence for God based on inference from the existence and nature of the universe. However if there is a God who is perfectly good and loving, then it may be expected that He will not only sustain the universe minute by minute but also on occasions intervene in His creation in special ways. These special occasions are often referred to as miracles and constitute a further argument for the existence of God. Whereas the earlier arguments focused on familiar and normal experiences, this argument focuses on events so rare and unusual that they are seen as signs of divine activity.

a) Miracles as interventions

This classic understanding of 'a miracle' focuses on the interventionist approach. A miracle involves some intervention by

God such that without that intervention, the event would not have taken place. The intervention is usually seen in terms of the breaking of a **law of nature**. Aquinas defined miracles, saying, 'Those things must properly be called miraculous which are done by divine power apart from the order generally followed in things.' He was one of the earliest philosophers to attempt to define a miracle, and distinguished between three kinds of miracles:

- Events in which something is done by God that nature could never do. E.g. the sun going back on its course across the sky.
- Events in which God does something that nature can do, but not in this order. E.g. someone living after death.
- Events that occur when God does what is usually done by the working of nature, but without the operation of the principles of nature. E.g. someone instantly cured of an illness that usually takes much longer to cure.

Probably the best-known expression of this understanding of miracles is by David Hume, who defined a miracle as:

A transgression of a law of nature by a particular volition of the Deity or by the interposition of some invisible agent.

Enquiry Concerning Human Understanding, 1777

However, two problem areas arise that may undermine the coherency of such a definition. One problem concerns the phrase 'laws of nature', whilst the other focuses on the nature of God. A coherent definition is one that makes sense and is logically consistent.

i) Laws of nature

- Does it make sense to say that a law of nature has been broken? The problem arises because of our understanding of laws of nature. If laws of nature are generalisations formulated retrospectively to cover what has happened, then there cannot be miracles. For whenever any event happens that is outside of the established natural laws, it would simply mean that we must widen the law to cover this new case. In other words, supposed laws of nature that are broken are better described as incomplete laws that need widening to incorporate the new happening. For instance, the natural scientist would argue that there is no reason for thinking that a particular law of nature has been supernaturally overridden. It's simply that the original law was wrong and now has to be adapted to include the new happening.
- Is it coherent to talk about laws of nature at all? If nature is to some extent random as modern science may suggest, then we can never know whether some law has been broken or whether things are happening in a natural but random way as opposed to a natural but ordered way.

- Alistair McKinnon argues that laws of nature are simply 'whatever occurs'. In his article 'Miracle and Paradox', in *American Philosophical Quarterly* 4 (1967), he says that laws of nature are:

  > simply highly generalised shorthand descriptions of how things do in fact happen ... Hence there can be no suspensions of natural law rightly understood. Miracle contains a contradiction ... if for natural law we substitute the expression the actual course of events ... Miracle would then be defined as an event involving the suspension of the actual course of events.

- Hume's phrase 'transgressing a law of nature' seems inappropriate. Laws of nature merely describe what will occur given a particular set of initial conditions. When those conditions are changed in some way, then the 'law' does not apply. When a miracle occurs, the initial conditions are different, since God's special activity is now also a new added condition. Hence the 'law' has not been transgressed.

ii) Nature of God

- To say that God intervenes in the working of the universe seems to imply a view of God as spectator of events. It suggests that an agent moves in where he had not been before. This is contrary to **classical theism** where God is seen as sustainer and preserver of the universe.
- If God is considered to be outside of time, then maybe it is incoherent to believe that a timeless God enters time and space and acts, since at that moment He would be limited to a time frame.

b) Miracles as having religious significance

Many think miracles need to hold some deeper religious significance than just breaking laws of nature. Richard Swinburne argued:

> If a god intervened in the natural order to make a feather land here rather than there for no deep ultimate purpose, or to upset a child's box of toys just for spite, these events would not naturally be described as miracles.

The Concept of Miracle, 1970

Certainly the Judaeo-Christian tradition supports this understanding where miracles are seen as signs from God. The word 'sign' is used in John's Gospel to refer to Jesus' miracles that always seem to point to something beyond the actual event. The gospel miracles were not seen as an end in themselves (cf Luke 10:13). However, the acceptance that God can intervene and that God is good does raise questions about the problem of evil and of a moral God. If God is all good and all powerful, then why are there so few miracles? Why doesn't God address the problems of the world more directly by means of miracles? What are we to make of a God who stands by and watches, as millions of people are led to gas chambers, yet who seemingly intervenes to heal an individual? Surely such a God would not be worthy of worship. Maurice Wiles expressed this tension in his book *God's Action in the World* (1986):

> Miracles must by definition be relatively infrequent or else the whole idea of laws of nature ... would be undermined, and ordered life as we know it would be an impossibility. Yet even so it would seem strange that no miraculous intervention prevented Auschwitz or Hiroshima, while the purposes apparently forwarded by some of the miracles acclaimed in traditional Christian faith seem trivial by comparison.

A God who acts in such a trivial way is, according to Wiles, a God not worthy of worship. This implies miracles do not happen if belief in a traditional God is to be maintained. However, this depends on prior beliefs about the nature of God. If there is other evidence that God is all-loving, then God may have reasons for acting as He does. For further discussion see Chapter 11.

c) Miracles as interpretations

Ray Holland presents a completely different point of view on defining miracles. His most often quoted illustration is of the boy in a toy car caught between the railway tracks with a train fast approaching and out of sight. The mother could see both the boy on the tracks and the train approaching. The train suddenly started to slow down even though the driver could not see the boy ahead. The train eventually stopped about a metre away from the boy, therefore leaving him unharmed. The mother looking on saw it as a miracle. She still said it was a miracle, even when she was later told that the reason for the train stopping was that the driver had had a heavy meal, suffered a heart attack and passed out, causing the automatic braking system to come into play and so stop the train.

Holland claimed that an event that has explanation within natural laws, nevertheless can be considered a miracle if it is taken religiously as a sign. Holland refers to this as a 'contingency miracle'. The presence of religious significance is sufficient, according to Holland, for a certain event to be termed a miracle. Reading Holland's account ('The Miraculous', *American Philosophical Quarterly* 2, 1965), it is not clear whether he was arguing that God actually intervened. On balance it seems that Holland wants us to think that it was divine providence that the driver fainted at that particular moment. William Craig, ('Creation, Providence and Miracles?', in B Davies [ed.], *Philosophy of Religion: A Guide to the Subject*), discusses how theologians have identified different types of divine providence, in particular the type that Holland may be expressing in his toy car illustration:

as Paul and Silas lie bound in prison for preaching the gospel, an earthquake occurs, springing the prison doors and unfastening their fetters ... God can providentially order the world so that the natural causes of such events are, as it were, ready and waiting to produce such events at the propitious time, perhaps in answer to prayers which God knew would be offered.

(p 152)

Others read into Holland's illustration a more **anti-realist** understanding. For an anti-realist, a miraculous event is an event that is a disclosure. It is not about a real action that a supernatural being has undertaken. It is an interpretation of an ordinary event. The event makes sense within the form of life of the religious believer and involves no 'real' actions of a God.

This approach had already been aired from the time of the **Enlightenment**. Whereas biblical scholars such as Reimarus (1694–1768) had argued that the Gospel writers had distorted the accounts about Jesus, or gave the miracles natural explanations (Jesus walking on a sandbank not on water), Strauss (1808–1874) introduced the idea of 'myth'. He did not challenge the Gospel writers' integrity but interpreted miracles in the light of first-century Palestinian culture, which Strauss saw as dominated by a mythical worldview. He did not regard miracles as actual historical events. Bultmann (1884–1976) developed this view, arguing that the mythological worldview portrayed in the New Testament was unintelligible and unacceptable. As far as miracles were concerned, they needed to be reinterpreted and their spiritual truths made clear.

There have, of course, been criticisms of this approach. Apart from its dismissal of the historical reliability of the Gospel accounts, this understanding of miracles is far removed from the more traditional definition demanding intervention by a supernatural God. Holland's approach can be seen as very subjective, since it relies on the viewer interpreting and labelling the event as 'miraculous'. It is not objective. It is a very personal assessment where an event has to be classed as miraculous if someone believes it to be so. Their naming it as a miracle makes it, by definition, a miracle. Those who criticise this approach are not necessarily denying that interpretation is important. They are claiming that miracles, if they happen, must have an objective reality.

2 Is it reasonable to believe in miracles?

The answer to this question depends on what definition we are accepting. If we accept Holland's interpretative understanding of miracles, then they occur whenever anyone so interprets an event as such. Most philosophical debate has centred on the more traditional understanding of miracles, particularly expressed by Hume. Although Hume's chapter on miracles in his book *Enquiry concerning Human Understanding* (1748) is scarcely 20 pages long, it is regarded as a major contribution to the debate.

a) Hume and the importance of testimony

David Hume wrote his famous chapter on miracles to demonstrate that no one could prove with certainty that a miracle had occurred. This served the purpose of undermining the use of miracles to demonstrate the truth of Christianity in particular, and religion in general. He did not deny the possibility of miracles since this would be contrary to the **empiricist** position, which was the basis of all his philosophy.

As an empiricist he believed that all questions of truth had to be based on experience, and which therefore involves an enquiry about evidence. Given that a wise person 'proportions' their belief to the evidence, and that laws of nature have been established and supported over a period of many hundreds of years, then it will always be more reasonable to believe that the law of nature has held and has not been broken, than to believe testimony claiming that the law of nature has been broken. In particular he noted that there were no equivalents in modern-day events that compared to the recorded miraculous events in the Bible. Hence he focused on testimony of others in the distant past. He concluded (*Enquiry concerning Human Understanding*) that their testimony could never outweigh our present-day experience of the regularity of nature:

> No testimony is sufficient to establish a miracle unless the testimony be of such a kind that its falsehood would be more miraculous than the fact which it endeavours to establish.

In particular he highlighted several reasons why testimony was less likely to be true. He argued that a miraculous event has never been proven to be true because:

- *No miracle has a sufficient number of witnesses.* What is required is a quantity of educated trustworthy witnesses to a public event. E.g. people who would have a lot to lose if found to be lying.
- *People are prone to look for marvels and wonders.* We all like ghost stories and recount them even when we don't believe them.
- *The source of miracle stories are from ignorant peoples.* This seems to be partly referring to uneducated Galilean peasants e.g. the Gospels). The miracle stories acquired authority without critical or rational inquiry.
- *The writers had a vested interest and so there was bias.* This was particularly the case if a miracle was being used to establish a religion (e.g. the Resurrection).

- *Religious traditions counteract each other.* This last argument is different from the other four. Unreliability here does not derive from the unreliability of the witnesses. Rather that the evidence is further contradicted by other witnesses. If an Islamic miracle supports Islam and so discredits Christianity as a true religion, then equally any claim of a Christian miracle will likewise discredit Islam. Hence evidence for one is evidence against the other and vice versa. This seems to undermine the evidence.

Hence Hume's conclusion that it was more rational to distrust the testimony about a miracle than to believe that the law of nature had been broken. Indeed some commentators would argue that Hume thought miracles were impossible. For a discussion on whether this is a fair conclusion see M Palmer, *The Question of God* (2001), pp. 182–183.

b) Responses to Hume

A number of responses have been made in reply to Hume's argument.

i) Hume and his empiricism
Hume argued that for an event to be counted as a miracle it must violate the uniform experience that makes up the law of nature. He also claimed that all the empirical evidence relevant to the law had confirmed it as having no exceptions. This seems to beg the question that surely one cannot say nature has been uniform unless the assumption is made that all miracles are false. Further, if it is argued that exceptions to law cannot be sufficient to overthrow the law, but rather the exception is unreliable – then how do laws ever change? Logically we should never accept an exception! And therefore never change a law!

ii) Probability
Hume seems to equate probability with 'frequency of event'. By their very nature one would not expect many miracles. If **naturalism**, as opposed to supernaturalism, is assumed, then miracles will be rejected. Those who are theists will be more inclined to see miracles as likely to have happened, since it would be consistent with their beliefs. For them it has little to do with 'how many' but more to do with God's nature and purposes. Wise people should base their beliefs on facts, rather than odds.

iii) The criteria for testimony
Many regard Hume's criteria for testimony as being too stringent. If applied consistently to all past occurrences, might we not have to give up the writing of history?

It is questionable whether Hume would ever have accepted any testimony for a miracle. He goes on to refer to instances of 'miracles' in France which supposedly took place during his lifetime. These were 'immediately proved on the spot, before judges of unquestioned integrity, attested by witnesses of credit and distinction, in a learned age in a cultured country.' Hume refused to credit such testimony on the grounds of 'the absolute impossibility or miraculous nature of the events which they relate' (*Enquiry Concerning Human Understanding*).

Hume writes as if all believers were either deceivers or the deceived. He fails to take into account the possibility that some people, including religious people, are by nature sceptics.

iv) The self-cancelling argument
The argument that miracles have a self-cancelling nature has been questioned on two counts. Firstly, some advocates of one religion will now often allow that a number of other religions have at least some elements of truth and may even have divine authority. Therefore miracles could occur in other religions.

Secondly, some argue that miracles can be performed by other sources than God. (e.g. evil forces), and these may be the sources of miracles in some other religions.

Even if Hume were right about the self-cancelling, it would not follow that the evidence for all miracles would be invalidated, for the evidence for the miracles of one religion might be much more impressive than the evidence for miracles in another.

v) Other evidence
Hume was writing at a time when the only support for a miracle came from a testimony. However, today we may be able to appeal to scientific evidence and so on. He did not consider the kinds of physical effects or traces which a miracle might leave, which might provide evidence for its occurrence independent of testimony. For instance, a healed withered leg stands as evidence, apart from the testimony of the one healed, or X-rays, photographs or videotapes.

3 Modern supporters

Amongst the most recent defenders of miracles are the philosopher Richard Swinburne and the physicist/theologian John Polkinghorne. Both argue that science does not prove that miracles are impossible or self-contradictory. In addition, Swinburne (*The Concept of Miracles*) argues the case that evidence for a non-repeatable happening, which breaks the law of nature, is acceptable historical evidence. This dismisses Hume's claim that the law of nature must always be the stronger evidence. The fact that God is the cause of the extraordinary event is strengthened if the event occurs in answer to a prayer and if it is an act consistent with the nature of God. Swinburne (*The Concept of Miracle*) also attacks the argument that when a law of nature appears to be broken it is either because we are mistaken or that we are not yet aware of the true law.

> We have to some extent good evidence about what are laws of nature, and some of them are so well established and account for so much data that any modification of them which we could suggest to account for the odd counter instance would be so clumsy and ad hoc as to upset the whole structure of science. (p. 32)

Indeed, it has been said that to salvage the law of nature requires just too many ad hoc adjustments. For example, the law of nature that people die and stay dead may be amended by the clause 'Except when the person's name begins with the letter J; he claims to be God and founds a major western religion.'

Such an approach for maintaining that laws of nature are never transgressed seems unreasonable.

The thrust of Swinburne's arguments is to show that it is rational to believe that a miracle has occurred, while allowing the possibility that evidence might turn up later to show that we are mistaken. He comments:

> 'We may be mistaken' is a knife which cuts both ways – we may be mistaken in believing that an event is not a divine intervention when really it is, as well as the other way around.

Is There a God? (1996) p. 121

Another recent defence of miracles has attacked the anti-realist, demythologising approach to biblical miracles. The book *In Defence of Miracles* (ed. R Geivett) contains a number of articles arguing the case for the historical reliability of the resurrection of Jesus. Certainly it is true that if you reject the supernatural, then you must reject the miracles as historical events. However, this seems a purely arbitrary decision since many argue that the strongest evidence for the supernatural is found in the Gospel accounts. They would claim that there are very good reasons for accepting the Gospels as historical documents. (e.g. Craig Blomberg, *The Historical Reliability of the Gospels*, IVP, 1987).

4 What might miracles prove?

a) Miracles show that God exists

Miracles have often been viewed as an inductive proof for the existence of God since they are consistent with the existence of God. It is the best explanation of certain irregular states of affairs.

The difficulties of this approach include:

● How do we identify an irregular state of affairs?
● How do we justify the introduction of the concept of God to account for such an event?
● Is Hume's understanding of miracles incoherent?

However, the arguments for God's existence can be seen to be part of a cumulative argument (see Chapter 9).

b) Miracles can show the authenticity of a revelation

Certainly the Judaeao-Christian tradition supports this view. For instance Hebrews 2:3—4:

> This salvation, which was first announced by the Lord, was confirmed to us by those who heard him. God also testified to it by signs, wonders and various miracles …

Miracles may function like a divine signature, confirming God's actual sponsorship of a particular revelation claim.

Swinburne argues that we should expect miracles, given that we expect revelation. Since God needs to communicate with His creatures, He needs to authenticate His revelation. God may be considered to exist via other arguments for God. Given that if God exists, miracles are not impossible – then attention focuses on the historical evidence for that miracle occurring.

Criticisms of this approach include challenging:

● the assumption that God probably exists
● the assumption that God is interested in giving revelation to His creatures
● the assumption that we can be sure about occurrence of miracles through historical investigation

c) Miracles reveal the nature of God

Miracles are an essential part of the actual content of the revelation. According to the Christian tradition, Jesus entered our world by means of the Virgin Birth. Jesus died but overcame death. His resurrected body was seen and touched by His disciples. When Jesus walked the earth, He came into conflict with evil and was victorious over it (the exorcisms etc). Prophecy is fulfilled. God acts through answering prayer and actively intervenes in and sustains the universe.

The questions raised about this approach include:

- Is the historical evidence sufficiently convincing?
- Is the **Incarnation** coherent with the nature of God?
- If Jesus is God, how can He die?
- Why does God intervene so few times and often in such limited situations (the problem of evil)?
- How can a timeless God intervene in time?

Answering questions on Chapter 8

Consider the following:

1. 'A miracle is an amazing coincidence of a beneficial nature.'
   'A miracle is an event of religious significance.'

Explain these two definitions of miracles.

Most candidates will refer to Holland's illustration of the boy in the toy car caught in the railway lines as an illustration of the first definition. This is a very visual story and examiners report that many candidates recount the story in lengthy graphic detail, and then omit to explain the point of the illustration!

In answering any exam question the following may serve as a useful checklist:

- Has the answer focused clearly on the issue of the question?
- Does the answer relate back to the question?
- Does the answer show evidence of one (two) year's study (e.g. correct use of technical terms and reference to named scholars)?
- Ask yourself, 'What does this fact illustrate?'
- Have I already illustrated that point?
- Have I explained the relevance of this material to the slant of the question?
- Does this add anything new to the argument?
- Can I express it in a more concise way?

One of the difficulties with questions about miracles, is that often the exam question will just refer to 'miracle' without defining it. As we have seen, there have been a number of different understandings of the meaning of the word 'miracle' and different definitions raise different issues. Hence it is important to state which definition you are using when answering.

For example:

2. 'Miracles cannot happen.'

Examine and assess this view.

Clearly the response to this depends on which definition is being considered. Remember that in evaluative questions, a sustained argument is required rather than a list of points. Again the level descriptors will indicate what is expected at the different levels. If only one side of an argument is given in the answer, then it is likely that less than half the marks available for that question would be the maximum that could be scored.

The value of theistic proofs

KEYWORDS

cumulative argument – a collection of arguments that together increase the persuasiveness of the case

cognitive statements – statements that have a truth value

non-cognitive statements – statements that are not open to truth or falsity at all

basic belief – a belief that is either self-evident, incorrigible (cannot be mistaken) or evident to the senses

blik – a framework within which events are interpreted

foundationalism – the view that beliefs must be supported by evidence or by basic beliefs

fideism – the view that certain beliefs are beyond the scope of reason and must be accepted on faith

1 Cumulative arguments

It is generally agreed that as deductive arguments (see Chapter 1) the theistic proofs fail. However, as has been noted, the recent approach sees them more as probabilities and inductive. In particular, Swinburne argues that 'the probability of theism is none too close to 1 or 0' (*The Existence of God*, pp. 290–291). In other words, he agrees that they are fairly evenly balanced. He then considers the Religious Experience Argument and sees this as making theism overall probable. Swinburne argues that his conditions have been met as regards his two principles (see Chapter 7), and no special considerations hold given that he has shown that the other theistic arguments cannot be classed as 'very improbable'. Hence he concludes that theism is more probable than not.

Certainly this type of **cumulative** approach has been used by others, though not in the specific form that Swinburne has used. Often appeal is made to the Occam's razor approach, which claims that unnecessary entities should be erased (hence 'razor'). Hence the solution to all the questions raised by the theistic arguments such as cause, order and regularity, and morality is the one entity, called God. This is regarded as a simpler solution since it only requires the single entity 'God' for a solution to *all* the arguments. However, whether the introduction of the entity 'God' is really a simpler answer has been challenged, given the complexities of the concept of God!

Also, none of the different arguments for God's existence prove that He is the God of classical theism. None the less, as Davis points out (*God, Theism and Theistic Proofs*, p. 188), if the beings proved to exist by the arguments 'are all one and the same being, then clearly we have arrived at the existence of a being that is remarkably similar to the God of theism'.

The usual cumulative argument takes the form of accepting that though each argument in itself is not a proof, the arguments when added together become more convincing. In other words, theism is the one solution that all the arguments point to and that most satisfactorily takes account of the wide range of data. Various analogies have been used to illustrate this approach. For instance, if you have a leaky bucket (inductive argument for God's existence) and insert other leaky buckets inside it (more arguments for God's existence), then the leaks are sealed (i.e. the arguments gain strength)! Others have been quick to point out that 0+0=0 (i.e. that a failed argument added to another failed argument results in both failing!).

Obviously the persuasiveness of the inductive arguments will depend on each of the separate arguments having some probability. John Hick sees the heart of the issue as a decision as to whether the universe is ultimately intelligible or whether it is a 'brute fact'. To people who believe the former, theism will appear a reasonable explanation.

2 Criticisms

Recent writings have seen an increasing attack on the whole idea of theistic proofs. This has come from a number of different angles.

a) Rationality

Richard Messer (*Does God's Existence Need Proof?*, 1997) notes that Swinburne assumes that his logical argument will convince any rational person. The assumption being 'that there is a paradigm standard of rationality to which people should adhere'. Messer suggests that the Wittgensteinian approach of conceptual relativity challenges Swinburne's assumptions. Swinburne is accused of making the judgement that all viewpoints other than his own are inadequate. In other words that the view that he, Swinburne, holds is what does actually constitute reality.

However, many like Wittgenstein would point out that our idea of what constitutes rationality depends on our 'conceptual frameworks and criteria for making judgments' (Messer, p. 121). How we interpret evidence depends on our already existing ideas. R M Hare coined the term '**blik**' to mean a framework within which events are interpreted. (For further discussion about bliks see below and Chapter 14.)

Alvin Plantinga is another modern-day philosopher who has challenged our understanding of rationality. He questions the basis of rationality which rests on 'foundationalism'. **Foundationalism** is the view that rational belief must either be supported by evidence or by **basic beliefs**. Basic beliefs are those beliefs that seem so obviously true that we feel compelled to agree with them. Hence basic beliefs must be either self-evident, incorrigible (cannot be mistaken) or evident to the senses. For example, if I believe I am in pain, then it cannot be false that I am in pain. This is a basic belief that requires no evidence or justification. Applying this understanding of rationality to the issue of a belief in God means that for rational belief in God, some evidence is required by the believer, since the belief does not fulfill the criteria for a basic belief.

Plantinga argues that theistic beliefs can be basic beliefs. He does this by raising two criticisms against foundationalism:

- Believing 'I had lunch yesterday' does not satisfy the basic belief criteria, yet it is a basic belief in that there is no reasoning taking place. I may use reason to repel a belief that my memory is faulty, but my belief is not inferred from my reasons for rejecting the view that my memory is faulty. Hence Plantinga shows that our criteria for basic beliefs are inadequate.
- Foundationalism itself does not meet its own criteria as a basic belief. The belief that 'all rational beliefs must be either basic or justifiable according to basic beliefs' is itself neither a basic belief nor justifiable in terms of basic beliefs. Hence according to foundationalism, foundationalism itself is irrational.

Plantinga is therefore arguing that we cannot say *a priori* what the criteria are for a basic belief. Rather we should try to identify common features of the basic beliefs that people have in their thought system. Plantinga maintains that belief in God is one such basic belief since it has the feature of an unfounded belief which provides the foundation for other beliefs. Hence belief in God does not require evidence to justify it, to make it a rational belief. It is a basic belief. A theist's belief in God is as rational as one's memory beliefs. Plantinga regards humans as having a natural capacity to apprehend God's existence on a par with our natural capacity to apprehend truths about the past. For a good critique of Plantinga's position see W Wainwright, *Philosophy of Religion*, pp. 155–159.

b) Faith and belief

Often a criticism is made along the lines of 'Well, if God was proven, there would be no room for faith'. The implication is that such a proof would devalue the importance of faith.

Indeed it is argued that a religious belief cannot be subjected to proof. In support of this view is often quoted a verse from Paul's letter to Corinth 'We walk by faith not by sight' (2 Corinthians 5:7). Faith is seen as a contrast to knowledge, implying that it is an area that is not totally certain. R M Hare argued that the religious believer does not make assertions that are either true or false but adopts 'bliks'. This is the principle by which we live and with which we interpret experience. Hare used the illustration of an Oxford don who was convinced that all the other Oxford dons were trying to poison him. Any examples of behaviour that suggested differently were seen as a subtle attempt to put him off his guard. Such belief is a 'blik' and nothing can count against it. It cannot be refuted by evidence because it helps to determine what counts as evidence.

This emphasis on faith rather than rational argument reflects the views of the philosopher Kierkegaard (1813–1855). He gave three arguments why reason played no part in faith:

- For the believer, faith in God was a statement of a certainty rather than a statement of mere probability. However, reasoning could never produce a certainty and so reasoning has no relevance to faith.
- Authentic faith requires a degree of commitment such that the believers do not imagine they will change their belief or abandon it. Reasoned argument could never produce such a commitment. Kierkegaard saw that what was required was 'a leap of faith', so that the belief would remain even when argument failed.
- Without risk there could be no faith. Indeed 'intense passion' is the essential feature of religious faith. This means that the greater the leap, the better the quality of the faith. Passion, for Kierkegaard, varies in proportion to the risk's enormity. The risk is greatest when faith's object is not just uncertain but absurd. Hence faith in the Incarnation, which Kierkegaard felt reason rejects as absurd.

The view that the central tenets of religions are not able to be shown to be the case by rational argument but must be accepted on faith, is called fideism. Most fideists do not deny that reason has a role in religion (though some do), but claim that faith precedes reason in matters of religion.

Karl Barth (1886–1968) is another example of someone who places faith above reason and so rejects the approach that focuses on weighing up the arguments for God. Barth's three main defences of this position are cited by J Webber (*Faith and Reason*, 1995):

- God can only be known through Jesus and anyone to whom the Son chooses to reveal Himself.
- Human reason is corrupted as a result of the Fall.
- Divine revelation is the ultimate criterion of truth, not human reason.

Hence 'Christian truths are revealed by God, and anything that is revealed by God is true irrespective of the findings of human reason.' (*Faith and Reason*, p. 20). However problems arise over judging between different religious claims of revelation, and the assumption that there is indeed a God who reveals.

For further discussion on belief/faith and evidence, see the next chapter.

c) Understanding of the word 'God'

Perhaps the strongest attack on theistic proofs has come from the area of philosophy of language. The assumption in the theistic proofs is that 'God' is an external, independent objective being. This is to regard statements about 'God' as '**cognitive**'. Cognitive statements are statements that are true or false in the ways that literal statements are true or false. However, other philosophers see religious statements as more '**non-cognitive**' (i.e. not open to truth or falsity at all). On this understanding, religious beliefs are not factual claims. A belief in the last judgment has nothing to do with events that will happen in the future. Rather it is reflecting about the meaning of life and death. Messer sums up the issue clearly (*Does God's Existence Need Proof?*, p. 51) with a quote from D Z Philips:

> Coming to see that there is a God is not like coming to see that an additional being exists. If it were, there would be an extension of one's knowledge of facts, but no extension of one's understanding. Coming to see that there is a God involves seeing a new meaning in one's life, and being given a new understanding.

Therefore the theistic proofs are seen to be irrelevant at best and a total misunderstanding of what 'God exists' means. There is no new fact to discover but rather seeing what is already here in a completely new way. To be an atheist is not about rejecting factual beliefs but more about rejecting a way of life. For further discussion of this approach see Chapter 14.

Answering questions on Chapter 9

Exam questions on the existence of God will often demand some discussion on the idea of proof, and so material in this chapter would be particularly relevant.

Remember to refer to the cumulative argument as a possible argument in favour of God's existence. Make a chart of the key points of the cumulative argument and then list reasons why some see this approach as a weak argument.

I. To what extent can the design argument for the existence of God be viewed as a reasonable argument?

This clearly involves some discussion about what constitutes a reasonable argument. An inductive argument always contains the possibility of leading to error since its conclusion does not necessarily follow from the premises (see Chapter 1). Reasonableness often involves risking a hypothesis as true in the light of other competing statements, as well as weighing up the probability of the evidence. However the failure to find a more probable competing hypothesis does not prove that there is none. Equally there remains a difficulty over how we individually weigh up what is more probable. This in turn is affected by our presuppositions.

2. To what extent does Kierkegaard show that faith is opposed to reason?

This is an evaluative question and so requires some sort of weighing up of the evidence besides just stating the evidence. A good answer will not just state a critique but will also respond to that critique. The discussion about Kierkegaard's three arguments might include:

- Is it true that faith requires certitude?
- Shouldn't religious believers be humble and open to correction?
- Should we believe in Santa Claus, as that requires strong faith?

10 **Faith and Reason**

1 Belief

> **KEY ISSUE** What is the relationship of reason and evidence to religious faith and belief?

It is important to understand what is meant by the word 'belief'. In everyday speech to say 'I believe something is true' is often taken to mean 'I believe that it is probably true'. However, in its more precise sense, the word 'belief' means 'I have a conviction that it is true'. That conviction is not necessarily there as a result of logical argument. Belief may come about by deductive argument, by inductive argument, by personal experience or even by sheer blind personal acceptance and prejudice.

2 Belief-that and belief-in

Firstly consider '**belief-that**'. A typical 'belief-that' statement is 'I believe that the Pope is the head of the Roman Catholic Church.' The statement is making a claim that is objectively true and that something is a fact. We call this propositional belief. A person believes that:

- Some state, process or thing exists independently of the actual belief that they exist.
- This belief is more likely to be true than any rival or alternative belief.
- The likelihood of one statement of belief being true as opposed to another rival statement being untrue lies with:
  - the statement is consistent with our general perception of what is true
  - the greater or more persuasive evidence for it; and
- The statement is true.

What counts as evidence for the belief will depend on the nature of the statement. The belief that there is a table in the room will be based on the senses. In contrast, historical statements will be evaluated differently.

The essential issue is that such evidence indicates that the truth of the belief is more likely than not, and more likely than alternative propositions.

These criteria are what we mean when we speak of a rational belief.

In contrast, an irrational belief can be described as a belief:

- for which the person has no evidence whatsoever
- which conflicts with or contradicts, and is known to do so, other well-grounded beliefs that the person holds
- which the person claims to know is false, while continuing to believe it
- for which the person claims there could never be evidence.

Now consider '**belief-in**' statements. An example of a belief-in statement would be 'I believe in Jesus', where clearly this usually means more than just belief that Jesus was an historical figure. It also implies trust in Jesus. Belief-in may be contrasted with belief-that, by saying belief-in conveys an attitude of commitment, trust, or loyalty on the part of the believer. This attitude, or psychological stance, forms part of the object of belief-in. It is, however, difficult to see these two as contrasts as it would be irrational to trust or be loyal to something one did not believe to exist.

Ludwig Wittgenstein (1889–1951) held a view of belief that reflected something of the belief-in understanding of commitment and trust. In his *Philosophical Investigations* (Blackwell, 1953) he stated:

> 'I believe' is not giving a report on my state of mind. Believing … is a kind of disposition of the believing person … shown … by his behaviour.

> *(II, 191)*

In this view 'belief' is seen not so much as a mental state, but more as a disposition to respond in certain ways to certain circumstances. For further discussion on Wittgenstein see Chapter 14.

3 Belief and evidence

There are some things that are easy to believe, such as 'The Queen lives at Buckingham Palace'. There are some things that are difficult to believe, such as 'The table is made up of atoms that have gaps between them'. There are some things that I can't make myself believe, such as 'The world is flat'. I can't make myself believe that because the evidence overwhelmingly implies the world is round. In other words we hold beliefs because there is some degree of evidence for that belief.

John Locke (1632–1704) argued that the only opinions that had a right to be held were those that had evidence to support them. William Clifford (1845–1879) expressed the same view even more forcibly when he wrote:

> It is wrong always, everywhere, and for anyone, to believe anything upon insufficient evidence.

Lectures and Essays, 1879

For Clifford there was a moral obligation about deciding what to believe, since poorly supported beliefs could harm other people. He gave an illustration of a ship owner who, though he had doubts about the ship's seaworthiness, nevertheless sent sailors to sea in it. He persuaded himself that the ship would be guarded against accident. As a result the sailors died as the ship went down in mid-ocean. Clifford argues that the man was guilty of the deaths of the sailors, 'since he has no right to believe on such evidence as was before him'. (*Lectures and Essays*). Equally if people accepted beliefs without any evidence, then they would be more likely to believe wrong things in the future and so harm themselves:

> Every time we let ourselves believe for unworthy reasons, we weaken our powers of self-control, of doubting, of judicially and fairly weighing evidence.

William James (1842–1910) responded to Clifford's views, arguing that it is right to believe in some cases where there is a lack of strong supporting evidence. When we are faced with choices that are 'living, forced and momentous' but lack good objective evidence, then we make our decisions with our 'passional nature'. In particular James sees the religious hypothesis as just such a choice. For a good discussion on this see Wainwright's *Philosophy of Religion* (1988), pp. 148—153.

As we saw in the last chapter (p. 75), Hare also challenged the role of reason for religious beliefs. He argued that the religious believer does not make assertions that are either true or false but adopts 'bliks', and so nothing can count against the assertion of the religious believer. However, this is challenged by those who point out that things do count against a religious belief (i.e. there is a weighing up of evidence, so arguments for God are relevant). For instance, if there were evidence that Jesus never lived, then one would have no right to believe that Jesus rose from the dead. Brian Davies (*Thinking about God*, 1985) makes a number of observations concerning belief and evidence (pp. 244—260), including the following:

- Not all beliefs are provable. Indeed if we are to believe anything at all, there must be inferred beliefs to start with.
- We are often entitled to belief without proof. For instance, believing things that people say to us if they are experts.
- Certain central beliefs of Christianity illustrate the problem of proof (e.g. Incarnational doctrine that Jesus is both fully human and fully God). One attempted solution has been to appeal to historical accounts of Jesus in the Gospels. However, even if we were to accept the accounts as accurate, 'an interpretation going beyond the evidence would still be required'. The issue is that the doctrine is not just a report of historical facts.
- Though we often use the word 'belief' of things open to doubt, we also use it of things we can prove, that we can give solid evidence for and regard as conclusively proved.

4 Faith

When trying to define faith, most thinkers have juggled between a mixture of will, propositional belief and trust. Aquinas worked from the premise that the Christian faith was fundamentally rational. As such, it could be supported and explored by reason, as Aquinas demonstrated with his 'Five Ways' (see p. 27). However, for Aquinas, the foundation is divine revelation, since reason alone could not discover the truths and insights of the Christian faith.

A McGrath (*Christian Theology: An Introduction*) identifies three components to Martin Luther's (1483–1546) concept of Christian faith:

- Faith has a personal, rather than a purely historical, reference. Belief in the facts, by themselves, is not adequate for true Christian faith.
- Faith concerns trust in the promises of God. Faith is not just about believing something is true but being prepared to act upon that belief.
- Faith unites the believer to Christ. Faith makes both Christ and his benefits – such as forgiveness, justification, and hope – available to the believer (p. 129).

As we have seen above, faith seems to include a belief-in, as well as a belief-that. Hence personal trust is often seen as an important element. An act of the will is used in deciding and abiding by that choice. Luther used the illustration of a boat:

> The person who does not have faith is like someone who has to cross the sea, but is so frightened that he does not trust the ship. And so he stays where he is, and is never saved, because he will not get on board and cross over.

(cited by McGrath, *Christian Theology*, on p. 127)

5 Faith and reason

Fideism is the view that central tenets of religions cannot be shown to be the case by rational argument, but must be accepted on faith. Hence reason has no place. However, such a view can be challenged. C Stephen Evans (*Thinking About Faith*, 1985) points out that:

> In a pluralistic culture it is almost impossible not to reflect critically on where one should place one's trust. (p. 20)

Also our ability to reason can be seen as a gift from God. Therefore it would seem right to use that ability when faced with a variety of conflicting religious claims.

A distinction is often made between believing something by faith and believing something by reason. However, this may be false. Faith is acting on what you have good grounds to think or know is true – a leap, but not a leap in the dark, or an irrational step. Often faith involves weighing the evidence. Basil Mitchell propounded a story about the resistance movement. A partisan meets a stranger whom he believes is the secret leader of the resistance movement. Sometimes the stranger appears to be working against the movement, but he is told that this is all part of the stranger's plan. The partisan continues to believe the stranger. Likewise religious belief continues, often when there seems to be contrary evidence. The believer weighs the evidence and assesses what is the most reasonable and consistent overall view. For instance, a Christian has faith in the love of God as shown by the Cross, despite the contrary evidence of suffering in the world. He would claim that such a position of faith was not unreasonable.

Evans (*Thinking About Faith*,1985) comments that:

> a faith which evades critical questions is a faith that lacks confidence, which is not truly assured it has found truth. (p. 177)

He argues that if God wants us to freely choose to love and obey Him, then God couldn't make it *irrational* to be a theist. Hence the theistic 'proofs' could be seen as one aspect by which we choose freely by means of our rational faculties.

6 Pascal's Wager

The French mathematician and philosopher Blaise Pascal (1623–1662) presents an interesting approach to religious belief. In 1654 he had a religious experience and became a devout Christian. Afterwards, by means of his famous wager argument, he tried to persuade his friends to give up their hedonistic way of life and become pious Christians. He argued that God couldn't be known by argument and evidence. The evidence for God is ambiguous. Equally Pascal did not see religious belief as a cold intellectual judgement (belief-that) but rather as an emotional, passionate conviction (belief-in). Hence argument alone could not produce that emotion of the heart.

As a result he developed what has become known as Pascal's wager. He argued that it was sound judgement to act as though there existed a God who grants eternal happiness to those who sincerely believe in Him. Pascal taught that those who sincerely sought God by living what he called the 'religious life' (e.g. living piously, going to Mass) would come not only to give intellectual assent to the existence of God but also to experience the reality of God in a heart-felt way. He believed that personal faith was the way to eternal life.

The wager involved a choice that could not be avoided in life. We have to choose either to live as though God existed or live as though God did not exist. Pascal argued that it is unreasonable to be an atheist. For if the theists were right, they would win eternal happiness as opposed to annihilation. What the theist would be giving up would be short-term pleasures of a life of self-indulgence and gratification. The atheist would have gained a life of pleasure at the cost of eternal happiness.

However, if the atheist is right, and there is no eternal happiness, then the theist will have lost some of life's pleasures. Yet the atheist gains little more – just a few pleasures of this life. Hence good judgement requires us to risk the wager (stake) of living pious lives. It appeals more to self-interest than to the truth of God.

Needless to say, many have questioned the logic of Pascal's arguments:

- Pascal offers the choice between God existing and God not existing. However, the actual choice is between the Christian God and no God. It does not consider the option that there might well be a God but not the one that Pascal was advocating. Hence the theist could still be condemned for following the wrong God.
- Pascal makes a step of faulty logic. He argues that there are a number of religions in conflict and therefore only one is true. However, a set of contrary beliefs do not demand any of them to be true. They may all be false.
- The persuasion of the wager assumes a God who will annihilate the unbeliever. However, what if God is forgiving? It would then give the atheist not only pleasures in this life but also eternal happiness with God in the next life!
- Pascal assumes that God will condemn those who have unbelief even though he accepts that the evidence for believing is not intellectually convincing. Surely it would be morally wrong of God to condemn those who cannot believe because they do not have the evidence?

● Would it not be morally wrong of God to reward those who only believe because of self-interest and greed?
● It is not guaranteed that living a life of faith as though one were a believer necessarily results in the faith that God requires. To act as if one believed does not guarantee that one will believe.
● If the wager is rejected, it is by no means certain that an atheist cannot become a Christian by some other means. Indeed there are countless examples of atheists becoming Christians by other means, so maybe to remain as an atheist, rather than live as though one were a believer, might be more likely to result in conversion.

Pascal never included the idea of hell (eternal damnation) in his argument. However, this would not change the argument. M Curd (*Argument and Analysis: An Introduction to Philosophy*, 1992) comments that it may be logically impossible for a perfectly good God to condemn anyone to eternal damnation, since it would be unfair to have an endless punishment for finite human wickedness. Also in terms of philosophical argument:

> It is not always irrational to choose an action that carries with it a slender chance of an infinite loss. (p. 76)

Answering questions on Chapter 10

The material in this chapter may need to be combined with the material in the previous chapter for general overview questions on faith and belief. For instance:

1. Assess the role of faith in supporting religious belief.

The coverage of material should include a variety of views with some critical analysis, as the question is evaluative. A negative view of the role of faith would see faith leading to beliefs that were without justification or even irrational. In this view, faith would be seen to have little value and the emphasis would be on reason. This could then be contrasted with a view that saw faith taking precedence over reason (e.g. Kierkegaard). Indeed some religious beliefs may be deemed to be beyond our reasoning and so require faith. If reason were sufficient, then there would be no room for faith.

Finally, it could be argued that faith and reason both have an important role to play in religious belief. Faith is supported by reason and is necessary to move the believer from the merely intellectual assent, to a commitment and trust relationship with God.

Evaluation involves expressing these different views with evidence and arguments. Some critical analysis should be attempted, such as identifying some weaknesses with the arguments, and through a process of reasoning, an appropriate conclusion should be reached.

11 The problem of evil

1 The problem stated

KEY ISSUE The so-called 'problem of evil' was first formulated by Epicurus (342–270), and has been restated in various forms down through the centuries. Augustine (354–430) in his *Confessions* expressed the dilemma as:

> Either God cannot abolish evil, or He will not; if He cannot then He is not all-powerful; if He will not then He is not all-good.

The assumption is that a good God would eliminate evil as far as He is able. Given that He is all-powerful, He should eliminate it all. However, evil exists. In other words God has the means (power) and the motivation (love, goodness) to eliminate evil. So why does He not do it?

When put in its simplest form it is seen as essentially a logical problem:

● God is omnipotent.
● God is all-good.
● God opposes evil.

Therefore evil does not exist in the world.

The argument seems to be valid, at least from a theistic point of view, in that believers in God would agree with the premises. However, most would admit that evil does exist. There is therefore a contradiction, and if one is to remain logical it suggests that one of the premises is wrong. However, that would deny classical theism. In one sense, the problem is really only a problem for the believer in God. If there is no God there is no problem.

It is usual for philosophers to include God's omniscience in God's omnipotence, for a God who can do anything but does not always know what is the best way of doing it, might be said to be less than all-powerful. Also it is usual to maintain that God cannot do the logically impossible, e.g. make square circles. Neither can He do what is inconsistent with His nature. However, it must be acknowledged that philosophers still debate these points. 'God is all-good' implies that He opposes evil and will wish to remove it. Attention is often drawn not just to the presence of evil in the world, but to whether the existence of God is compatible with the amount of evil in the world.

The illustration of evil is an important aspect of clarifying what the 'problem of evil' actually is, since different types of evil raise different philosophical issues. It is usual to divide evils into :

- **Moral** – which arise from the responsible actions of groups and individuals who cause suffering or harm. They include such things as stealing, lying and envy, as well as the evils of some political systems.
- **Natural** – which arise from events which cause suffering but over which human beings have little control eg earthquakes and disease.
- Some make further groupings such as **physical** – which refers to pain itself and mental anguish – and **metaphysical** – which refers to imperfection and contingency as a feature of the cosmos.

At various times certain events have been used as classic illustrations of evil. At one stage it was the Lisbon earthquake of 1755, but in the present day it is the Holocaust that illustrates moral evil, and AIDS or cancer that illustrates natural evil.

A further issue is the actual origin of evil. If God created or caused all things then clearly He is the originator of evil. The fact that God is all-powerful and so all-knowing also raises problems about our free will and hence responsibility for doing evil. Also the fact that God is the originator and doer of evil implies that followers of God should copy His example.

The problem of suffering highlights a slightly different emphasis. It focuses on the *experience* of the evil. It raises different questions because of the experience. It deals with the problem on a more personal level, i.e. how does the individual respond to suffering? The questions that are raised here are more of the form: Why me? Why now? Why this particular form? Why this intensity? Why this length? These seem to be questions that struggle to find purpose and explanation in what is being experienced.

Quite clearly, the rather academic and cold discussion about the philosophical problems of evil are often inappropriate for someone battling with their own personal pain and grief, and this raises questions of whom the discussion is aimed at. Possibly most discussions have been levelled at the atheist, and an attempt has been made to show that evil is not logically incompatible with the existence of God. Such attempts include Swinburne's 'free-will defence' which particularly concentrates on the problem of the *amount* of evil. In contrast, others focus on the moral issue, assuming God exists but unsure whether one can trust such a God. Such a stance is found in the character of Ivan Karamazov in Dostoyevsky's novel *The Brothers Karamazov* (1880). Likewise John Roth's 'protest **theodicy**' is addressed to such an audience. Yet another audience are believing theists who want to understand why God allows evil. Such books as C S Lewis' *The Problem of Pain* (1940) fit this category. As I said earlier, being in anguish does make a difference to how one approaches the problem of evil and many books have been written from this perspective. *A Grief Observed* (1961, Faber & Faber) is a classic book by C S Lewis about the death of his wife.

It is important to recognise the different audiences to whom the writings on the problem of evil are addressed, since they are written for different purposes, to achieve different results. Hence in assessing an argument, it seems unfair to accuse it of saying nothing about some issues, given that it was only attempting to address another issue, and unfair therefore to conclude that what it says is worthless.

Many have argued that there is a contradiction involved in the fact of evil and the belief in an omnipotent all-loving God. However, it does not seem logically contradictory, since it is not the same as saying 'there is a God and there is no God'. It is not logically necessary that an omnipotent all-loving God prevents evil, and a **theodicy** is an attempt at a solution of the problem of evil, without denying God's omnipotence or love or the reality of evil. It shows how God is justified in allowing evil. The word *theodicy* is from the Greek *theos* meaning God, and *dike* meaning righteous. Alternatively, a defence argues why it is reasonable to believe that God has reasons to allow evil without actually demonstrating that those are the reasons.

Hence theodicy could be defined as a philosophical and / or theological exercise involving a justification of the righteousness of God. Clearly this justification requires the theodicist to reconcile the existence of an omnipotent, omniscient and morally perfect divinity with the existence and considerable scale of evil.

I think if I were to try and state what all the theodicies share in common in their solution, it would be that evil is a necessary condition or consequence of some otherwise unachievable good, which God desires to create. This could be summarised as all being justified by some kind of greater good, e.g. free will or a maturing process.

a) Does evil exist?

One approach to the problem of evil is to deny the problem by denying the existence of evil. Monism states that everything is of one nature. Assuming that this nature is good rather than evil, it means that evil is an illusion. Monists would acknowledge that we may 'feel' that such a view of reality is false since we 'seem' to experience evil. However, our feelings are false.

In reply Ninian Smart (*Philosophers and Religious Truth*, 1964, p. 140) commented that even if 'from the standpoint of eternity' we are mistaken in our imaginings of suffering, we will still have experienced what other people would regard as real suffering.

b) The nature of God

Another approach to the problem would be to challenge the nature of God: either His goodness or His omnipotence.

i) God is not all good / loving

This suggests that God is generally unconcerned about destroying evil and so presents a rather sadistic picture of the character of God. Clearly this is not the God of classical theism because it requires God to be morally imperfect.

However, recent writings, e.g. John Roth (in *Encountering Evil*, Ed. Stephen Davis, 1981) and Elie Wiesel (*The Trial of God*, 1979), particularly in the aftermath of the Holocaust, have seen the development of a 'Protest Theodicy'. Given God's omnipotence, events in history like the Holocaust demonstrate that such a wasteful God cannot be totally benevolent. In the foreword to Wiesel's play *Trial of God* he recounts an occasion when he saw three rabbis put God on trial in Auschwitz, found Him guilty and then went off to pray. It is that sort of tension that this theodicy advocates. In a sense it is not a new response since it follows the pattern set by Abraham, Moses and Job, all of whom contended with God. The Psalms are full of protest to God (e.g. Psalm 90). Nevertheless despair is not the response, but rather a defiance of God, reminding Him of His promises and a risky hope for the future.

Such an approach has brought forth criticisms such as whether a God depicted by this theodicy is worthy of worship.

ii) God is not omnipotent

This would provide a solution by recognising that God is incapable of destroying evil. For instance, dualism argues for two co-eternal substances locked in conflict and that the continuance of evil is indicative of the lack of power of God. Certainly such a view can be found in ancient mythologies of Greece and Rome and contributed to the belief that matter (e.g. the body) was evil.

A modern form of this approach is called 'Process Theology'. Amongst its proponents are A N Whitehead and David Griffin. The problem of evil is removed by redefining the meaning of omnipotence. It is a reaction against the classical Christian theodicies in which God seems unaffected by our suffering, even immune to it and this world and its experiences are seen as relatively unimportant. The emphasis in salvation on escaping from this realm illustrates such views.

In contrast, Process Theology stresses this life and maintains that the most real thing about a person is the series of experiences which make up the process of their life here and now. God is seen as one intimately involved with this world and its suffering. Indeed, God is called a 'co-sufferer'. The different understanding of God's omnipotence derives from Process Theology's view that creation was not *ex nihilo* (out of nothing). Rather, creation was the achievement of order out of a pre-existing chaos. This limits God's power since these pre-existing materials are not totally subject to God's will. Hence God is depicted not as a powerful, almighty despot but rather as someone who creates by persuasion and lures things into being. God is in time and both affects and is affected by the world. He even depends on His creatures to shape the course of His own experiences. Such a God cannot control finite beings, but can only set them goals which He then has to persuade them to actualise. Evil occurs when such goals are not realised. Natural evil is also explained. For instance, Griffin states, 'If cancerous cells have developed in your body, God cannot lure them to leave voluntarily'. (in *Encountering Evil*, ed. Stephen Davis, 1981).

Needless to say, such a view has not passed without criticism. It is seen as a major departure from the God of classical theism. Certainly it is admitted that there is no guarantee that good will ultimately overcome evil. It is not even clear that there is life after death, and some process theologians speak in terms of existing in the memory of God.

2 The two classical theodicies

> **KEY ISSUE** In Western history there have been two main theodicies, those of Augustine (354–430) and Irenaeus (130–202).

a) The Augustinian theodicy

It should be noted that Augustine approached the problem from different angles; his various thoughts on the issue can be found in a number of his writings including *The Confessions* and *The City of God*. It is difficult to conclude exactly what Augustine's answer was since he had strands of thought rather than a worked-out theodicy. For a good account of this, read Bernard Farr's article in *Dialogue*, Issue 1.

The central theme of Augustine's thought is that the whole creation is good. It is also a realm that has great variety of forms of existence, each having its appropriate place in the hierarchy of being. As God is the author of everything in the created universe, it follows that evil is not a substance, otherwise it would mean that God created it, which Augustine rejects. Thus for Augustine, evil is a 'privation'. A privation is the absence or lack of something that ought to be there. It is the malfunctioning of something that in itself is good. For instance, sickness is a real physical lack of good health. Evil cannot exist in its own right. Evil enters when some member of the universal kingdom, whether high or low in hierarchy, renounces its proper role in the divine scheme and ceases to be what it is meant to be.

God created *ex nihilo* (out of nothing) as opposed to 'ex Deo' (out of God). God cannot be less than perfect but his created beings can be destroyed or deprived. God cannot be the author of this corruption, so for Augustine the answer is found in free will. It is good to be free but with that freedom comes the capability of actualising evil. Augustine argues for a belief in the fall of angels and of man. God foresaw man's fall 'from the foundation of the world' and planned their redemption through Christ. In Augustine's writings it seems clear that he saw the angels that fell as predestined by God to do so. In the case of man he sees that through Adam, all are in a state of guilt and condemnation but God brings some to repentance and salvation.

Figure 3 - The Archangel Michael hurls the rebellious angels into the abyss, Giordano, 1650

From these general ideas have stemmed a number of variations so that it is usual to refer to theodicies that use Augustine's main ideas of privation, the fall and free will as 'Augustinian type theodicies'.

i) Criticisms of Augustinian-type theodicy

- Modern science rejects the picture of a fall of humanity from perfection. Rather it suggests an evolutionary development. A literal approach seems to contradict modern science. Hence some have taken the book of Genesis as a symbol / myth depicting the fact that all humans do sin, by choice.
- If humans are finitely perfect, then even though they are free to sin they need not do so. If they do then they were not flawless to start with – and so God must share the responsibility of their fall. (Note that Augustine argues that some angels were predestined to fall. If this view is not accepted then how did angels fall, given that they were perfect?) Surely in a perfect world they would have no reason to sin? In response, it is argued that God could have brought about a world where creatures were free but never sin, since Jesus was free to sin and did not. Alvin Plantinga (*God, Freedom and Evil*, 1974) argues that it is logically impossible for God to create another being such that it by necessity freely performs only those actions which are good. For God to cause them to do right would be a contradiction of their freedom. Others have argued along different lines, pointing out that even if it is logically possible, not everything logically possible is actually achievable. Love cannot be programmed. The fact that heaven is pictured as containing people who will never sin suggests that perhaps God could have created such beings on Earth. However, we will have chosen to be in heaven which may entail some restrictions to our free will as a result.
- It is hard to clear God from responsibility for evil since He chose to create a being whom He foresaw would do evil. Many see 'love' as the key to this issue. God wishes to enter into loving relations with His creatures. But genuine love is an expression of the free commitment of both parties. Love between God and His creatures is therefore possible only if the creatures are free – that is, if they are able to reject His love as well as respond to it. Without freedom we could not share in God's goodness by freely loving Him. Nevertheless, the creation of free creatures involved the risk that persons would misuse their freedom and reject the good, and this is what happened. God could have chosen to make a world without free creatures in it. This would mean that the creatures would be robots, and therefore it would be a non-moral world. It may be physically better but it cannot be regarded as morally better, since it is non-moral.
- The existence of hell is not consistent with an all-loving God. Hell seems contrary to a loving / good God. As a result some argue that all are saved whilst others suggest annihilation rather than eternal damnation and suffering.

● Augustine's view of evil as a privation is challenged. It is not sufficient to say that it is a lack or absence. Many would argue that it is a real entity.
● If everything depends on God for its existence, then God must be causally involved in free human actions. Do we have free will?

b) The Irenaean theodicy

In general terms, the Augustinian theodicy is a **soul-deciding** theodicy. In contrast, the Irenaean theodicy is **soul-making**. In the writings of Irenaeus (130-202), there appears the idea that humans were not created perfect but are developing towards perfection.

Irenaeus distinguished between the 'image' and the 'likeness' of God (Genesis 1: 26). Adam had the form of God but not the content of God. Adam and Eve were expelled from the Garden of Eden because they were immature and needed to develop, i.e. they were to grow into the likeness (content) of God. Thus they were the raw material for a further stage of God's creative work.

John Hick (*Evil and the God of Love*, 1968, p. 290) commenting on this further stage, says:

> ... it is the leading of men as relatively free and autonomous persons, through their own dealings with life in the world in which God has placed them, towards that quality of personal existence that is the finite likeness of God ...

The fall of humanity is seen as a failure within this second phase (likeness), an inevitable part of the growing up and maturing. The presence of evil helps people to grow and develop. Thus the emphasis in this theodicy is *soul-making*.

Irenaeus himself never developed a full theodicy as such, but his approach represents the type put forward by Friedrich Schleiermacher (1768–1834), and in more recent times by John Hick. Hick sees the first phase of God making man in His image, as the culmination of the evolutionary process, whereby a creature has been evolved who has the possibility of existing in conscious fellowship with God. The second phase involves an existence of making responsible choices in concrete situations. It is a necessary pilgrimage within the life of each individual.

The value of this world is:

> ... to be judged, not primarily by the quantity of pleasure and pain occurring in it at any particular moment, but by its fitness for its primary purpose, the purpose of soul-making.

Evil and the God of Love (1968), p. 295

Hick goes on to argue that:

> ... in order to give people the freedom to come to God, God creates them at a distance – not a spatial but an **epistemic distance** (a distance from knowledge of God). He causes them to come into a situation in which he is not immediately and overwhelmingly evident to them. (p. 317)

In other words the world is ambiguous and it could equally well be reasoned that there is no God as strongly as there is a God.

An essential part of this theodicy is that this process is worthwhile because of the eventual outcome. If the process is not completed in this life, then Hick argued that there is another life in another realm to which we go, until the process is complete.

The reason why God creates imperfect rather than perfect beings is twofold according to Hick:

● Human goodness that has come about through the making of free and responsible moral choices, in situations of difficulty and temptation, is more valuable than goodness that has been created ready-made.
● If humans had been created in the direct presence of God they could have no genuine freedom. Hence the epistemic distance. It is best that free beings freely choose to love God.

The Irenaean-type theodicy also has an element of 'greater goods'. For instance, some moral goods are responses to evils and hence could not exist without them, e.g. courage, compassion, forgiveness. Sometimes this is referred to as a 'second-order good'. The moral goods are those that result from alleviating, resisting and overcoming evil and involve intelligent and informed responses to evils. This could be seen as a necessary part of the soul-making process.

i) Criticisms of Irenaean theodicy

● If the end result is guaranteed by God, what is the point of the pilgrimage? Indeed, if there is universal salvation then do we have free will to refuse to mature? Some point out that we could forever refuse, while others comment that there is infinite time. This issue of the end result being realised is crucial to the theodicy. If the end result is not realised then how can the evil experienced be justified?
● Does the end justify the means? The suffering experienced (e.g. Auschwitz) cannot justify the ultimate joy. Indeed, in the Holocaust, people were ruined and destroyed more than made or perfected. It is hard to see how this fits God's design and human progress.
● Could not the greater goods be gained without such evil / suffering? For instance, cannot cooperation be learnt by teaming together to win an athletics match?

● As a Christian theodicy, it seems to make the atonement superfluous and unnecessary. The response is that Jesus is an example to show us one who has the content of God. Perhaps a more Christian approach would be to see the theodicy more in terms of 'faith-making' than 'soul-making'.

● A number of criticisms involve suggestions of better ways to achieve this process. For example, why did the natural environment have to be created through a long, slow, pain-filled evolutionary process? Why could an omnipotent God not do it in 'the twinkling of an eye'? Equally, if we go on to another life to reach maturity, then why did God not simply make our earthly spans much longer, so that we could reach the Celestial City on earth, or at least get closer? Indeed, is there any evidence for other lives? (see Chapter 13).

c) The free-will defence theodicy

Implicit to both the Augustinian and the Iranaean theodicies is the free-will defence. It is argued that the evil that exists in the world is due to humanity's misuse of the gift of free will. God wished to create a world in which created rational agents (i.e. human beings) could decide freely to love and obey God.

Recently Swinburne (*Existence of God*, 1979) has addressed the problem of the sheer quantity of evil, which many feel is unnecessarily large. He points out that a genuinely free person must be allowed to harm herself and others. God could intervene to stop her or let her learn from consequences. However, the latter is more in keeping with the exercise of moral freedom. What of free choice to bring about death? Swinburne argues that death is good in that it brings an end to suffering. It would surely be immoral for God to allow humans to have unlimited power to do harm. Also actions matter more when there is a limited life. Death makes possible the ultimate sacrifice, it makes possible fortitude in the face of absolute disaster. When it comes to the Holocaust he says 'the less God allows men to bring about large scale horrors, the less the freedom and responsibility he gives them'. In other words, we can make real choices.

For Swinburne, natural evil is necessary so that humans have a knowledge of how to bring about evil. Rational choices can only be made in the light of knowledge of the consequences of alternative actions. He cites the example of earthquakes. A choice of building on earthquake belts, and so risking destruction of whole populations, is only available if earthquakes have already happened due to unpredicted causes (*Existence of God*, p. 208).

d) Pain and suffering

Hick comments that the removal of pain in a material world would require:

… causal regularities to be temporarily suspended … and would approximate to a prolonged dream in which our experience arranges itself according to our own desires.

Evil and the God of Love (1968), pp. 341–342

One can intend to harm someone only if one thinks it is possible to do so. Richard Swinburne has argued that an intention to cause harm supposes the knowledge that certain sorts of behaviour will cause harm and an appreciation of what pain, mental anguish, and other harms are like. As we have seen, some argue that suffering is sometimes necessary for a higher good to be achieved, e.g. courage.

Attempts at understanding pain and suffering will be dependent on which theodicy one favours. Those in the Augustinian tradition would see it as the result of the fall of man and the consequence of rebelling against God. Shouts of 'Why doesn't God do something?' receives the reply of 'God has' – in that the Cross is the ultimate solution. God has reversed the effects of evil both here and now, and ultimately. The Bible suggests that linking your life with God starts putting evil in reverse, so that in heaven pain and suffering will be totally absent.

Another Biblical idea is that God suffers with us. He is with us in our suffering. Also the omnipotent God can turn evil and suffering to good account.

Alternatively, the Irenaean tradition sees it as necessary for soul development. It is through suffering that character and virtues are often developed. The Old Testament story of Job describes him as suffering as part of a test. The test is whether he will continue to love God, in spite of his sufferings. The outcome is that Job ceases to look for an explanation – it is sufficient to experience God. On an individual level this is the Christian approach to coping with pain and suffering, recognising that it is a Christian responsibility to work for the removal of evil.

e) Natural evil

J S Mill said in *Three Essays on Religion* (London: Longmans Green) that:

> Nearly all the things which men are hanged or imprisoned for doing to one another, are Nature's everyday performances. Killing, the most criminal act, Nature does once to every being that lives!

The Augustinian tradition would argue that our rebellion against God has affected all of creation and distorted it, so that our environment is not as God intended it (Romans 8: 22). In addition Augustine saw natural evil caused by fallen angels who by their free decisions wreak havoc.

Others note that things like volcanoes and earthquakes are in themselves neutral. Like a powerful waterfall, there is nothing inherently evil in them. Rather they become evil when people are hurt by them. Hence some have argued that if we had remained in perfect fellowship with God, then God would guide us away from these dangers, and hence we would not be hurt by them. In this case they would not be regarded as evil. An illustration of this is of a three-year-old child living near a busy road or deep river. Both are life-threatening but, close to and protected by her parents, both road and river can be a source of usefulness and life.

In contrast the Irenaean theodicy sees natural evil as the best possible agent for the purpose of soul making. It is also part of the epistemic distance.

f) Animal suffering

Reconciling animal suffering with a good God causes many people the most difficulties. This is because it seems to have no connection with free moral actions, nor brings about a greater good. Attempts at a justification include:

- Denial that animals feel pain.
- Animals are different from humans in that we recall past and predict future, hence reflect on our suffering.
- Most animal sufferings occur when they are removed from their natural habitat. C S Lewis develops this idea in his book *The Problem of Pain* (1940).
- Pain is not useless. Although animals do not have a moral nature to develop, they are physical and pain can act as a warning system.
- The natural order has been affected by the fall of man and perverted animal life.
- In some way animals serve the soul-making process, possibly by contributing to the 'epistemic distance' by which man can exist as a free and responsible creature – free to harm God's creation.
- Natural selection aids evolution.

g) Conclusion

Are the theistic responses adequate? Certainly many people find the existence of evil a persuasive argument against the existence of God. It is an issue that affects every one of us and so moves beyond the merely academic interest.

Answering questions on Chapter 11

Try drawing up a list of points of (i) comparison and (ii) contrast between the Augustinian theodicy and the Irenaean-type theodicy. A good summary of this to check against can be found in John Hick's *Evil and the God of Love*.

This topic covers a large amount of data. It is vital that you do not just regurgitate that material regardless of the question. Exam questions have a clear focus so that candidates can be tested on the important skill of selecting relevant material. However, all questions will require an allusion, to a greater or lesser extent, to the actual 'problem' raised by the existence of evil.

Consider the following questions:

1. 'If God were the omnipotent, wholly good, creator of all things, then evil would not exist. Evil exists. Therefore, God is not the omnipotent, wholly good, creator of all things.'

    Examine this argument.

2. 'The problem of evil never can be satisfactorily solved.' Discuss.

In the first question there is a danger that the candidates will not make specific reference to the particular quote given. The logic of the quote needs to be explained. God has both the means and the motivation to remove evil. Also some discussion about the phrase 'evil exists' is required. The claim that evil does exist could certainly be challenged. The conclusion will be challenged by the theodicies. As always with the topic, there is a danger that breadth will be chosen in preference to depth and as a result a 'list' approach develops rather than debate and evaluation skills.

If Process Theodicy is referred to, remember that it denies the omnipotence of God and therefore changes the classical form of the argument.

Question 2 requires a statement of the problem of evil. Remember that this is more than a mere statement of its logical form. There is the issue about the origin of evil; and the types of evil (moral/natural) pose problems of their own, e.g. why create a world with earthquakes in when they are so harmful to humans?

When referring to the solutions, it should be made clear how that particular theodicy solves each of the problems identified in the first part of the essay. Remember that every discussion essay must contain evaluation.

12 The mind and body problem

1 Mind and body?

Before discussing the issue of life after death (Chapter 13), it is necessary briefly to consider the nature of humans. Our views about the different models relating mind and body will influence our views about personal identity and what constitutes a person. This in turn will affect the way we understand such concepts as resurrection and reincarnation.

Human beings appear to be characterised by both body (physical) and mind (consciousness) properties. Your body can be defined as the mass of matter whose weight is your weight. It has size, shape, mass and spatial and temporal position. It is composed of recognised material stuff such as carbon. It has physical properties such as height. Your height is a fact, whatever you may think about it. It is independent of a person's conception, or their mental processes.

An example of a mind property would be thinking about your height, or self-consciousness. This is dependent on your conception. The characteristics of mind include 'qualia' and 'intentionality'. **Qualia** is qualitative rather than quantitative. It concerns felt experiences like tasting a hamburger. John Puddefoot (*God and the Mind Machine*, 1996) explained qualia as 'properties of the inside-out world that cannot be seen from-outside-looking-in'. Intentionality means 'aboutness': I don't just think, I think *about* something. In contrast it does not seem sensible to speak about tables directing their attention on an object. They have no attention to direct! It is because of these sorts of properties that many philosophers make a distinction between body and mind. The problem is whether mind and body are one and the same nature (monistic) or whether we do have two natures (dualistic). If they are two separate entities, then a further problem arises as to how they interrelate.

2 Dualism

> **KEY ISSUE Dualism** has been the prevalent view. Dualists argue that people have composite natures, namely material and non-material.

The non-material element is usually called the soul, spirit or mind. It should also be stated that many argue for soul and mind being different, in that the soul represents the spiritual aspect of man, whilst the mind is more linked to the brain and related to reasoning etc.

The Greeks saw the body as a tomb or prison of the soul. The ultimate destiny of the soul was to be released from the body. This sort of idea is inherent in the Hindu idea of reincarnation, where the aim of the soul is not to be reincarnated into another body, but to be absorbed into the oneness of God (Brahman). In contrast the traditional Christian view is expressed in terms of a resurrection of the body. The relationship envisaged could be phrased as 'My body is my soul's proper home. My soul is my body's proper master'. (Arthur Custance, *The Mysterious Matter of Mind*, 1980, p. 81). However it should also be noted that recent Christian thinking has tended to emphasise the person as a whole (holistic) and hence has moved towards a more monistic understanding.

a) Descartes

The classic presentation of dualism is by Descartes. He argued that the body is spatial and in no sense conscious, whilst the mind is non-spatial and is conscious, having thoughts, feelings, desires, etc. As regards the interrelationship of the body and mind, Descartes favoured interactionism. This holds that states of consciousness can be causally affected by states of the body, and states of the body can be causally affected by states of consciousness. In other words, the mind and body can interact. An example would be drugs changing my perceptions and a nightmare causing me to scream out. Descartes further reasoned out that the point of interaction was in the brain. To be more precise, he sited it in the pineal gland, the one structure in the brain that is not duplicated. As to how these two natures interact Descartes remained agnostic.

The problem posed by the idea of something non-spatial causally affecting something spatial was deemed so severe that alternative dualistic models were proposed. Parallelism held that the mind and body are like two clocks, each with its own mechanism and with no causal connection between them, yet always in phase, keeping the same time. One clock had face and hands but no bells to strike the hours whilst the other had bells but no face or hands. To an onlooker it would seem that there was a causal relationship between the two clocks since the bells of the one rung when the other showed the hours. However, it is because they were regulated and ran in parallel that they exhibited a harmony. Parallelism proposed a similar idea for the harmony of the mind and body. The regulator was seen to be God.

b) Epiphenomenalism

Another variation is **epiphenomenalism**. This holds that bodily events can cause mental events. However, mental events cannot cause physical events, i.e. the mind cannot control the body. Indeed, what happens is that the mind is a by-product of brain activity. Electrical impulses move between brain cells and produce 'thinking', 'imagining', etc. Thinking etc. is not the electrical impulse. The mental is 'above' (*epi*) those more fundamental processes (*phenomena*) of brain events. A popular analogy is that of a shadow to the person. The shadow cannot affect the person. The causation is one-way.

Support for dualism has come from the work of the neurosurgeon Wilder Penfield and his research on epileptic patients (*The Physical Basis of Mind*, 1950). Exposed brain tissue of conscious patients had electrodes applied to it. The result was a double consciousness. They were aware of their immediate surroundings and of vivid re-enacted scenes from their past. Penfield concluded that 'if we liken the brain to a computer, man has a computer, not is a computer' (p. 108). Further weighty support for dualism has come from the work of Sir Karl Popper and Sir John Eccles. Although they differ as to the origin and destiny of the mind, they both argue for interactionism in their book *The Self and Its Brain* (1977).

c) Conclusions

Even if there are two natures, it could well be that both perish at death. Indeed, it would be odd that given their interaction, one should be mortal and the other immortal. Alternatively one may argue that given two natures of very different kinds, it would be odd not to consider that one might survive death.

Clearly the relevance of dualism for life after death is that it becomes a possible concept that our soul / mind / spirit does not cease when our body decays. Rather it can have an existence of its own or can be reclothed. Whatever it is, it suggests that something that is 'us' could continue on at death. Evidence from extra-sensory perception and near death experiences would add support to this view. For further discussion see Chapter 13.

3 Materialism

> **KEY ISSUE** This view argues that so-called mental events are really physical events occurring to physical objects.

Recent years have witnessed severe criticism of dualism and a rejection of the illusive and illusory non-material other self. One of the most famous attacks on dualism came from Gilbert Ryle in his book *The Concept of Mind* (1949). He described Descartes' model as 'the ghost in the machine'. The 'ghost' is the mind and the 'machine' is the body. He was indicating that he did not think that the mind, as a separate entity and nature, existed. Ryle rejected the idea of the mind as a different kind of thing from bodies. He believed such misunderstanding came about because of a **category mistake**. By this he meant that brain and mind belong to different logical categories which have been wrongly associated together. An illustration that Ryle used to clarify the phrase *category mistake* was that of a foreigner visiting Oxford or Cambridge for the first time and being shown a number of colleges, libraries, departments and offices. He then asks, 'But where is the University?' Ryle points out that this 'was mistakenly allocating the University to the same category as that to which the other institutions belong' (*The Concept of Mind*, Ch. 1). He searches for the University (mind) but is presented with colleges and libraries (body). The mistake is that he searches for the University as though it were a separate entity, when in fact he had already found it.

a) Philosophical behaviourism

The alternative theory that Ryle argued for was *philosophical behaviourism*. This saw all supposed 'mental' events as really a way of referring to a complex pattern of behaviour. He sees the term 'mind' functioning as a collective noun, like 'University', and so mind is no longer something internal but now comes to mean what we do with our bodies. We say someone is depressed because of the behaviour pattern they show, i.e. it is **materialism** because mental terminology actually means something physical (behaviour).

The obvious difficulty arises when a person in a particular mental state (e.g. wishing) does *not* behave in any particular way. This is overcome by introducing the concept of a disposition to behave, where appropriate behaviour is regarded as potential and can be anticipated given certain circumstances. Thus 'wishing' can be analysed in terms of physical behaviour even though it is not translated on every occasion into actual behaviour.

Most feel that this is an inadequate approach as an answer to the mind / body problem. Although it may be possible to refer to other people's mental states by reference to behaviour, it surely fails when we refer to ourselves. When I say that 'I feel pain' I am not referring to the way I behave. Furthermore, not all mind states can be expressed as behaviour states. For example, what of someone who pretended? There would be no difference in behaviour between the person who believed and the person who pretended to believe. Also it does not seem to answer the problem of our own self-consciousness – something that does not show itself necessarily in any behaviour pattern.

b) The identity theory

An attempt to overcome these difficulties is the **identity theory**. Instead of trying to analyse the meanings of mentalistic terms, it argues that mental and physical events are one and the same. The names 'mind' and 'brain', whilst having different meanings, nevertheless refer to the same object. A popular example concerns the offices of the vice-president of the United States and the president of the United States Senate. They do not have the same meaning but they do refer to the same individual. When I say 'I have a pain', I do not mean the same thing as when I say 'I have such and such a neural process'. However they are identical. Certainly the developments in neurosurgery that link a thought / action with a particular part of the brain, has popularised this theory of the mind / body relationship.

The major philosophical attack on this solution revolves around Leibniz's law of identity. This maintains that if things are identical then they must share identical properties. Thus opponents draw attention to such things as a wicked thought (mind), noting that a brain state (body) cannot be said to be wicked, and therefore Leibniz's law is not obeyed. In response the supporters argue that Leibniz's law does not apply to intention states. A wicked thought is an intention state since it refers to a particular way of representing, thinking or conceiving that thing.

c) Functionalism

The most recent approach to the mind / body problem is called **functionalism**. Analogies with computers are made where the software descriptions centre on their function. So in the same way, mental states can be defined in terms of their function (job description) or causal role. For example, the function or job description of pain is as a tissue damage detector. Pain inputs include tissue damage and trauma. Pain outputs include groans and escape behaviour. Thus all mental states can be seen as having a causal role. The concept of the mental state is therefore of an internal state caused by certain sensory inputs and causes certain behavioural outputs. It is this sort of model that makes some researchers of Artificial Intelligence argue that computers can think.

d) Conclusions

So what are the implications of materialism?

- **Moral responsibility**: It is difficult to see how free will is compatible with the theory that all brain events are physically determined. However, Donald MacKay (*The Clockwork Image*, 1974, p.79) argues that it is possible. He speaks in terms of 'logically indeterminate'. By this he means that even if it were possible to know all factors that caused brain events and be able to predict future action, it would still mean that the actual action could be different. The reason is that if that prediction were made known to the person, they would not be under constraint to follow it. The eventual outcome would thus result from a decision and therefore could be deemed to involve 'responsibility'. In reply it is said that in fact even this decision is ultimately physically determined and is merely an illusion of freedom.
- **Nature of the universe**: Do we live in a causally enclosed physical universe or is there a metaphysical realm? For discussion of the paranormal, see page 113.
- **Life after death**: Dualism seems to favour survival more than does materialism, when continuity after death is considered. Those who favour materialism have often argued for a Replica Theory approach where the whole person is recreated after death. For discussion of this see page 108. The interesting philosophical question that arises from such a view is whether 'the recreated person can be accurately described as being the 'same' person they were before they died'.

Hence it is necessary to consider briefly the issue of personal identity.

4 Personal identity

This is important for the philosophical approach to the study of life after death. Two issues in particular emerge:

- What criteria are there for deciding exactly what constitutes a person? Can what makes a person be isolated and identified?

● What are the criteria that are necessary for somebody to be regarded as the *same* person? For instance, if someone ceases to be, then reappears, what has to be true for the reappearance to be regarded as the same person as the one who ceased?

Philosophers have tried to tease out these criteria by inventing various scenarios that attempt to isolate exactly what constitutes a 'person'. By varying the scenarios it is possible to examine whether the characteristic that is isolated is the essential ingredient that makes a person a person.

Possibly the classic illustration originates from John Locke. He told the story of the cobbler and the prince where the two characters appear to wake up with each other's body. The 'cobbler' woke up in the palace and wanted to explain that he had not broken in but could not explain how he got there. However, he had the appearance of the prince. Meanwhile the 'prince' woke up in bed next to the cobbler's wife and accused her of kidnap and demanded to be taken back to the palace. He had the body of the cobbler. The problem is how to decide which is the cobbler and which is the prince. Which ingredient counts – the body or the memory? To which do you attach the person? Is it a case of bodily transfer or memory transfer?

Certainly the body lends itself to being a suitable means of verifying who a person is. The boundary of our skin clearly separates us from the rest of the external world. Our body also has continuity through space and time. However, the above illustration casts doubt on our certainty in identifying people in this way. Many feel that the body is not the essence of a person.

Again, another famous illustration is taken from Franz Kafka's story *Metamorphosis* (1916), in which the main character Gregor is transformed into a beetle. Does Gregor still exist? Certainly many regard this illustration as suggesting that the 'person' is the mind. Is my body 'me' or 'mine'? Is a brain transplant the only case where we would prefer to be donor rather than recipient?

Perhaps the reaction of self-interest is a clue to our view of personal identity. For instance, would you be happy stepping into a transporter machine that destroyed every cell but identically copied them at arrival. And what if the machine went wrong and produced lots of duplicates of you!?! Science fiction has been a great source for such illustrations. John Hosper's book *An Introduction to Philosophical Analysis* (Fourth edition, 1997) has excellent examples on this in Chapter 6. See also *How To Live Forever* by S Clark (1995).

For many the concept of a person is more than just a living human being. What of people who suffer from Alzheimer's disease? Often partners and relatives claim that they are 'not the same person'. Yet is Descartes' description of a person as 'a thinking thing' really sufficient? Is a robot a thinking thing? If so, is a robot a person? As has been mentioned, the conclusions about personal identity will be very much influenced by views about models of mind and body. Clearly it is also a vital issue when assessing views about life after death, and whether a 'person' survives death.

These are the main suggestions of criteria for personal identity:

- **Body**: there is continuity, though it is accepted that it changes with time. For example, if John is the same person today as he was yesterday, there must be continuity between the two. John's body gives him that 'continuedness'. However, resurrection and reincarnation do pose problems for this view.
- **Memory**: certainly this is what is unique about each individual and it also enables us to relate to our yesterdays, though what happens if I forget or have the wrong memory? Many philosophers argue that you need physical identity to verify memory, otherwise how can it be known that it is the same person?
- **Brain**: research on the brain by, for example, Penfield has suggested that each hemisphere has a separate consciousness with its own sensations, perceptions, learning experiences, memories, etc. If the two parts were transplanted into separate skulls, would both be the same person? For further discussions about this see Jonathan Glover's book *The Philosophy and Psychology of Personal Identity* (1988).
- **Personality**: a problem with this suggestion is that people have multiple personalities, so which one is the 'real' person? Recent research suggests independent centres of control within a person and so counts against any idea of unity.
- **Personhood**: perhaps the 'I' is flexible and consists of a number of things, such as rational thought, consciousness, self-consciousness and emotions.
- **Soul**: this is a similar idea to personhood with the addition of freedom and moral responsibility, relationship to God and determination towards supreme value. The soul finds deepest fulfilment in seeking a growing union with the supreme reality of God. Its proper purpose and true nature lie beyond the physical universe. A popular analogy is of a butterfly emerging from a chrysalis – it may be able to disentangle itself from properties of the brain and exist in a new mode.
- **Non-owner**: this is a radical approach that suggests that the word 'I' does not refer to anything apart from a stream of experiences that 'I' is supposed to own. As Hume said, 'I can never catch myself at any time without a perception, and never can observe anything but the perception.'

It should be noted that these criteria are not necessarily mutually exclusive.

Answering questions on Chapter 12

Most exam questions on this area in philosophy of religion are linked to life after death, so this chapter needs to be read in conjunction with Chapter 13. Both the various theories of mind and body, and the issue of personal identity, are important issues when considering philosophical problems about life after death.

A typical question set on the mind and body problem topic is:

1. **a)** Select and discuss the characteristic features of the relationship between mind and body. **b)** Discuss the influence of these views on arguments for life after death.

In (a) knowledge of a range of ideas would be expected. For instance dualism regards the mind and the body as different categories. In sharp contrast is Ryle and Behaviourism.

These differing models of the relationship between mind and body lead to different notions of life after death. Hence it is important that this chapter is read in conjunction with Chapter 10. For instance Dualism clearly favours immortality of the soul. Both reincarnation and resurrection need to be discussed. Hick's 'Replica' theory is also relevant with its view of the psycho-physical unit. A discussion of this material can be found in Chapter 13.

13 Life after death

KEYWORDS

disembodied existence – an existence without a body

'Replica' theory – the theory that an identical recreation of a person constitutes them being regarded as the same person

dualism – a fundamental twofold distinction, such as mind and body

reincarnation – the transmigration of the soul from body to body

ESP – extra-sensory perception

telepathy – the communicating of mind with mind

cryptomnesia – the memory of the subconscious

1 The philosophical problems of life after death

a) Is it meaningful?

Linguistic philosophy challenges whether it is even meaningful to talk of life after death. Flew suggested that the concept of life after death was contradictory. In his essay 'Can a man witness his own funeral?' Flew likened the phrase 'surviving death' to 'dead survivors'. To classify the crew of a torpedoed ship into 'dead' and 'survivors' is both exhaustive and exclusive (i.e. it covers all possibilities and no one can be in both groups). Likewise with 'surviving death'- it is self-contradictory and therefore meaningless.

Schlick claimed that it was not only conceivable but also imaginable that you could witness your own funeral. Flew challenged this by arguing that if 'you' are viewing your funeral, then what you are witnessing is not 'you' but your body (an empty shell). In a sense this is playing language games and does not deny the meaningfulness of life after death. A dualist (see page 99) view would answer both of Flew's criticisms.

In his essay in *New Essays in Philosophical Theology* (1955), Flew argued that words such as 'you', 'her', 'I', 'Peter' are person words referring to physical organisms and have meaning only in this context. They indicate actual objects which you can point at, touch, see, hear, and talk to. Thus it is non-meaningful to apply such words to either an immaterial or a spiritual body newly created by God. However, A J Ayer (*The Central Questions of Philosophy*, 1976) commented that there is 'no reason why the meaning of words should be indissolubly tied to the contexts in which they were originally learnt'.

Paul Badham (*Immortality or Extinction?*, 1982) questions whether the personal pronoun 'I' is a person word in quite the same sense as Flew's other examples. He argues that 'there is a real difference between our subjective experience of our own selfhood and our objective experience of the individuality of others' (p. 17). Science fiction stories involving body transfer illustrate the concept of 'I' remaining 'I' though clothed with a new and different body. Reported out-of-body experiences also display the concept of selfhood being applied to something other than the body (see section on evidence for life after death, p. 112).

A J Ayer commented that:

> If there could conceivably be disembodied spirits, the fact that it would not be correct to call them persons would not perhaps be of very great importance'

> *The Central Questions of Philosophy* (1976)

Confusion in language does not automatically mean that the concept being expressed has no reality.

b) Continuity

Advocates of materialism (see section on the mind/body problem, p. 101) face a major difficulty since there is nothing that could continue through death. If nothing continues then in what sense can one say that it is the 'same' person after death? The only solution would be for the body to be recreated. MacKay (*The Clockwork Image*, 1974) draws an analogy with a chalk message written on a blackboard and then erased. Just as the message can be rewritten using chalk or some other material, or even spoken, so God could recreate us after death (p. 78–79). The criticism is that nothing survives of the original entity, so in what sense can it be considered the same? It would be more accurate to refer to it as a replica.

i) John Hick's 'Replica' theory
Indeed, the '**Replica' theory** is one that John Hick argues for, following on from his theodicy of the 'vale of soul-making' (see section on Problem of Evil, p. 92). Hick acknowledges that there is a problem about continuity, but through three examples he argues that it is meaningful to call it the same person if someone dies and appears in a new world with the same memories etc. He uses the word 'replica' in inverted commas because he uses it in a particular sense – namely that it is not logically possible for the original and the 'replica' to exist simultaneously or for there to be more than one 'replica' of the same original.

He cites three examples in his book *Death and Eternal Life* (1976):

● In the first instance:

> Someone suddenly ceases to exist at a certain place in this world and the next instant comes into existence at another place. However the person has not moved from A to B by making a path through the intervening space, but has disappeared at A and reappeared at B.

Hick uses the illustration of London and New York:

> The person who reappears is exactly similar, as to both bodily and mental characteristics, as to the one who disappeared. There is continuity of memory, complete similarity of bodily features such as fingerprints, stomach contents and also beliefs and habits. The person would be conscious of being the same person though would not understand how they now come to be in a different place.

Hick argues that it is reasonable to call this person the same person as the one who disappeared.

● In the second instance, the person in London dies and a 'Replica' of him appears in New York. Again Hick argues that it would be reasonable to regard the 'Replica' as the same person who died – odd though it would be!
● The final case involves the person dying and reappearing in a different world. Hick likens this to waking up from sleep. The person then would regard themselves as the same person as the one who had died.

Hence by these progressive examples, Hick argues for the idea that a living person ceases to exist at a certain location, and a being exactly similar to him in all respects subsequently comes into existence at another location – namely in the next world. In this instance Hick argues that it is valid to say it is the *same* person. For Hick, a person is an indissoluble psycho-physical unity and therefore the body is a necessity.

In response, philosophers such as Terence Penelhum have challenged such a conclusion, arguing that there can only be an automatic and unquestionable identification when there is bodily continuity. As soon as this is lost, then it is debatable whether it is correct to call the two people the same person. This would raise the further problem of the appropriateness of divine judgement on such a being.

ii) Dualism
Dualism fares better since it allows for mental continuity. However, it involves isolating the 'ghost in the machine'. By definition it is not physical and therefore elusive. Popper saw the self-conscious mind having a personality 'something like an ethos of a moral character.' (*The Self and Its Brain*, 1977). R Zaehner has suggested that Hindus in

meditation experience not God but their naked spirit (*Concordant Discord*, 1970). However, most see the memory as the key to continuity. Terence Penelhum (*Survival and Disembodied Existence*, 1970) expresses it formally as 'the person A at time T2 is the same person B at some earlier time T1 if and only if, among the experiences that person A has at T2 there are memories of experiences that person B had at T1' (p. 77). The problem with such a view is that most people would argue that they were more than just the sum total of their memories. (see earlier section on Personal Identity for fuller discussion of the 'I', p. 103).

In contrast, **reincarnation** involves the idea of the transmigration of the soul (in the sense of the conscious character and memory-bearing self) from body to body, in other words, the 'I' who is now conscious, has lived before and will live again in other bodies. It involves a different body and no guarantee or need to remember past lives.

The problem that arises is in deciding in what sense it can be said that we keep our identity and have continuity. Many would respond by saying that it is irrelevant since what is important is the continuing development of the soul / spirit. However, without memory or bodily continuity in what sense are we able to say that the reincarnated person is the same person as the one who lived 500 years previously?

Another problem that arises is exactly who the person is who has been reincarnated. Supposing that this is the third reincarnation. Which person of the three are you?

c) Identification

Another philosophical problem involves the awareness after death of who we are and to what extent others will recognise us. Linguistic philosophy argues that the only possibility of identifying a person is to indicate some bodily criteria. However, at death the body decomposes and ceases to be. It is true that bodily criteria are necessary for identification in the conditions of the world in which we now live. Nevertheless that does not prove that they are therefore necessary when these earthly conditions are absent. Indeed, it is difficult to understand what would be meant by 'the same body' after death. During our lifetime we all change physically. Indeed, our very cells change.

Some have suggested that in the resurrection world we shall have bodies which are the outward reflection of our inner nature but reflect it in ways quite different from that in which our present bodies reflect our personality. If so, presumably people would recognise us. Perhaps God would ensure that others recognised us.

People such as Terence Penelhum have pointed out that even physical identity is no guarantee of identity. He quotes the fictional story of the cobbler and the prince (see page 104). This raises the problem of what criteria we use to identify and is a particular problem for reincarnation theories.

Of course, it is a questionable assumption that identification is relevant after death.

d) What kind of life?

Here the difficulty lies in applying our normal concepts of personal life to a post-mortem being. As regards resurrection – although the modern tendency in Christian theology is to regard man as a psycho-physical unity, there may be a strong case to retain the dualist view with the mind / soul surviving death and being clothed in a new body. An alternative would be to argue that the individual continues to exist in the mind of God between death and resurrection.

The New Testament gives an indication of the form of the resurrected body, if we regard Jesus' resurrection as a prototype. It could be touched and bore resemblance to the earthly body (Luke 24: 39). Yet at times it was not recognisable (Luke 24: 13-32). Also it was not limited in the way that our bodies are, for instance it could pass through matter (John 20: 19) and disappear (Luke 24: 51).

Some do not regard Jesus' resurrected body as the final spiritual body. Support for this is found in John 20: 17 which suggests that the ascended body was different. Also Paul likens the relationship of the earthly, physical body to the spiritual body using the analogy of the seed to the full-grown plant (1 Corinthians 15).

However, if Christians are in a physical, resurrected state and physical environment, will they have to queue to see Jesus? Where will this physical existence be? And what will they be doing all the time? Similar questions are raised about hell, though there is a modern tendency to reject this concept and favour annihilation.

Clearly the disembodied survival raises more problems than the doctrine of a resurrected body, since all the physical elements that make up our lives are inconceivable without a body. Disembodied persons cannot walk or talk, though psychical research and out-of-body experiences may suggest otherwise (see section on evidence for life after death, p. 112). The cases which tend to arouse the most interest among psychical researchers are not the cases where spirits are alleged to move physical objects, but cases where they are alleged to communicate by speaking through the mouths of mediums. This suggests the possibility of spirits occupying the bodies of people for short periods.

Out-of-body experiences suggest physical abilities through mental states, but this happens in a physical realm where items have form. If nothing had form (only mental states) then the difficulty about the type of life may remain.

The most famous work in this area is by H H Price (*Survival and the Idea of "Another World"*, 1952). He argued that perhaps the next world is not in space. Instead it could consist of internal processes only – a dream world, where each person would have their own private dreams. However it could still contain real communication and interaction with other minds e.g. ESP. The mental images acquired during the embodied existence would presumably be the source of the dreams. From the person's point of view the world would appear 'real' and 'solid' and existence may well appear to be bodily. However, the sequence and arrangement of events may be discontinuous as they are in our dream world, since the post-mortem world would be governed by laws of psychology rather than of physics.

If the next world is fashioned by our desires, then it may not be pleasant. They might reveal our true characters, including those that have been repressed. Ultimately this could be repugnant to our better nature. Hence we could develop our desires into something better and move to higher moral worlds.

John Hick (*Death and Eternal Life*, 1976) argues that if the mental worlds are created by our desires then it may be that many people will exist in isolation with no communication with others. In these cases he questions the quality of life and asks whether this is really 'living'. However, he solves the problem of the non-identical private worlds by suggesting the creation of a common shared world from everyone's mental images. All are pooled to produce a common environment, each contributing but not exclusively. Hick likens it to a superimposition of a great number of individual photos. However, this would be forever changing as new sets of desires were added with each new 'dead' person 'arriving'!

The alternative would be a number of separate worlds, as Price suggests. This could lead to highbrow and lowbrow worlds and worlds with endless philosophical seminars. Yes, we could be talking *real* heaven or hell!

Perhaps the major problem is that such views about the afterlife are not seen as consistent with traditional Christian teaching. Heaven is a world that is given to us and for us. It is not something that we create ourselves. However, Hick does argue that the mental image world could fit with his theodicy of soul-making, though not the final state.

2 The evidence for life after death

KEY ISSUE On a gravestone in York, there is an inscription that reads:

Remember friend when passing by,
As you are now so once was I.
As I am now you will be.
Prepare for death and follow me.

Underneath someone has scrawled:

To follow you I'm not content,
Until I know which way you went.

a) Psychic evidence

The belief in life after death has come under attack from various quarters. Modern advances in the sciences have seemingly supported a monistic and natural world view rather than a dualistic and supernatural one. Equally, the growth of secularisation has led to a rejection of traditional religious beliefs. One area of evidence to support life after death comes from psychical research.

In 1882, the Society of Psychical Research was founded to investigate evidence for the paranormal (known also as parapsychology). This area is relevant to life after death as it supports dualism and suggests that the power of the mind is such that thoughts and actions can be transmitted between the living and the dead. Evidence from such research can be divided into five main categories.

i) Telepathy

This is the name given to a thought in our mind being 'picked up' by another without normal communication. In 1934 Dr Rhine at Duke University in America published the results of tests based on the use of Zener cards (*Extra-sensory Perception*, 1934). Zener cards are a pack of 25 cards showing five each of several simple symbols: plus sign, star, circle, square and three wavy lines. These were shuffled and turned over one at a time by a 'sender' while a 'receiver' tried to guess the cards as they were turned. Similar results have been obtained by other researchers, though various criticisms are raised about the actual experiments and the interpretation of the data.

John Hick (*Philosophy of Religion*, 1983) concluded that 'it is difficult to deny that some positive factor and not merely "chance" is operating' (p. 129). This factor is referred to as **ESP** (extra sensory perception).

ii) Psychokinesis

Dr Rhine also made a study of psychokinesis (PK). This is the ability to move objects using the power of the mind. Helmut Schmidt, Rhine's successor at Duke University, produced a machine for testing this ability. The random appearance of an electron caused one of a series of bulbs arranged in a circle to light at random. The task of the PK subject is by the power of the mind to light the bulbs in order. Experiments seem to indicate that some people have succeeded. One of the most spectacular PK demonstrations said to have taken place involved a Russian housewife, Nelya Mikhailova, who separated the yolk of an egg from its white. A more recent example is Uri Geller who has convinced some that he can bend metal spoons, whilst others regard him as a very skilled stage magician.

iii) Spiritualism

Both telepathy and PK are seen to support spiritualism where, through a medium, contact is said to be made with the afterlife, for, if it were possible to pick up messages from other living people's minds, then it may be possible to pick up messages from the spirits of the dead. Also the spirits of the dead may be able to affect physical objects in our world by means of something akin to PK. The name 'poltergeist' (literally noisy spirit) refers to the occurrence of such a phenomenon. Needless to say this whole area has been rife with fraud. Some classic cases are recorded by Arthur C Clarke (*World of Strange Powers*, 1985). Investigation into spiritualism was one of the main reasons for the formation of the Society for Psychical Research.

In considering the possibility that someone who has died may communicate with the living in this way, we are presuming the continued existence of that individual as a persisting consciousness and will, a still-living personal being. We are supposing her to be carrying on a career of some kind in the next world, and in the midst of this occasionally to take time to visit her equivalent of a medium.

We are assuming therefore that the dead have a real life of their own, continuing to develop through time as persons. However, such a picture is lacking, according to John Hick (*Death and Eternal Life*, 1976). The spirits do not seem to speak out of the context of a continuing life; they seem to lack a credible environment of their own, a community of which they are a part, real next-world tasks, interests and purposes. They seem to be very much what they were in this world. And for this reason Hick argues that they are not spirits from the next world but more akin to residues of memory and traits that persist after death and that some people are able to 'pick up' ie residues from this life, not the next world.

Other possible alternative explanations of spiritualism include:

- **Telepathy** – the information given by the medium is gained by ESP from the living, not the dead.
- **Evil spirit** – this is the traditional Christian view, arguing that the spirit contacted is a masquerading evil spirit whose aim is to confuse and mislead people about the afterlife and God.
- **PK** – poltergeists are really the unconscious PK abilities of a living person in close proximity to the manifestation.

Equally many explanations for 'ghosts' have been offered. Some suggest that when a violent event occurs (e.g. murder) an unknown force is generated to form a 'psychic image' at the place where the event happened. The image continues to exist by absorbing energy, such as heat, and can be seen by people sensitive to the psychic force.

Alternatively ghosts are explained as delayed telepathy. If the mind has an independence of time, then it could pick up vivid pictures from the minds of people from the past.

iv) Near-death experiences

Out-of-body experiences (OBE) are cited as evidence of the spiritual element (soul) existing in its own mode without the body. Often this experience seems to occur to some people who have been near to death, or even been declared dead but then resuscitated, and are referred to as near-death experience (NDE). According to Hick, common elements of the experience include 'a sensation as of being drawn through a tunnel-like space' and of approaching a border but 'being sent or drawn back to the earthly body' (*Philosophy of Religion*, 1983). Cases cited by Paul Badham (*Immortality or Extinction?*, 1982, Chapter 5) show the accuracy of descriptions by patients as though viewing from above and looking down on their own body.

One of the earliest popular books on this subject was *Life after Life* by Raymond Moody (1975), in which he coined the phrase 'near-death experience'. It was this book that really brought this topic to the public forefront. Although accounts bear similarities across cultures there are also some clear cultural differences. In particular, Carol Zaleski (*Otherworld Journeys*, 1988) researched cases of medieval NDEs. She found that the subjects were obsessed with the pain of hell and included vivid accounts of being eaten by dragons and attacked by serpents and toads. Also there were accounts of 'test bridges' where the person faced an ordeal to be allowed to cross them. These seem clearly to reflect cultural influence and, whatever else they may be, they are not simply literal accounts of the afterlife. Many argue that NDE does not show life after death since the subjects are not dead, only near to death. Explanations suggested to explain this phenomenon include:

- Change of blood pressure can evoke a floating sensation.
- Oxygen reduction to the brain can cause hallucinations.
- Psychological response – a defence mechanism to disassociate our selfhood from our dying body.
- The effect of seemingly looking from above is really the creation of our world from memory.
- Accuracy of accounts may be due to ESP or knowledge of hospital life.
- The dark tunnel effect is the dim memory of transit through the birth canal.

To counter such naturalistic explanations, various accounts are cited of children recognising 'dead' relatives in the afterlife, of whom they had no previous knowledge. Peter Fenwick of the Institute of Psychiatry has commented that pilots do not recount NDEs when they suffer loss of oxygen in simulation practice. Equally, when the brain is disrupted you do not get clear vision or coherency. For a defence of NDEs as a real spiritual event see *Life after Death* by Farnaz Ma'sumian (1995).

v) 'Remembered' lives

This can be a spontaneous remembering, though the most dramatic evidence has come from hypnotic regression. Arnall Bloxham has produced some well-authenticated examples of subjects recalling details of past lives. Under hypnosis, subjects have taken on a different personality, speaking with different voices and sometimes even in a different language. Also some of the historical details, when checked, have been found to be accurate and not the sorts of details that the subject would be expected to know.

Ian Stevenson has investigated numerous cases suggestive of reincarnation and for a good critical account of his studies see Chapter 3 in *The After Death Experience* by Ian Wilson (1987).

Again, various explanations have been proposed:

● Cryptomnesia – this is the memory of the sub-conscious. Details of a historical period could have been absorbed from films and books. The mind can weave a fantasy around them.
● Genetic inheritance of the information.
● Telepathic sensitivity to the 'psychic husks' of some deceased person and identification with them.

However, as stated earlier, many would regard a mere persistence of some isolated cluster of memories as a denial of what is meant by survival after death.

b) Jesus' resurrection

Christianity expresses belief in an afterlife and claims that evidence can be found in the New Testament in the account of the resurrection of Jesus. Alternative explanations for the resurrection accounts include:

● New Testament accounts are symbolic and mythological rather than literal.
● The reports are late and one-sided and events were inaccurately remembered or passed down.
● The disciples had hallucinations.
● It was not Jesus who was crucified.
● Jesus did not die on the Cross but was in a coma and later recovered.

Counterarguments of orthodox Christian scholarship are that:

● Writings of the New Testament can be dated within the lifetime of witnesses. For example, I Corinthians was written within 25 years of the death of Jesus.
● Although written from within the Christian Church, they are written with apparent sincerity.
● The writers seriously claim that the events are historical and produce arguments for their historicity.

Figure 4 - 'The Resurrection of Christ', Master of Hohnforth, c. 1350

At the very least they claim that there is a historical case for the resurrection to be answered.

To those who already believe in the existence of a God of love, there are very strong grounds for believing that His intention is not our extinction. Keith Ward also argues that a Christian is committed to belief in immortality because of the existence of a God of love.

> The whole life of faith is one of trusting that the love which we fitfully apprehend in this life will be clearly seen hereafter.

Holding Fast to God (1982), p. 120

Answering questions on Chapter 13

The following are examples of typical questions on this area.

1. Discuss the view that evidence for life after death is so flimsy that the belief that it will happen must be wishful thinking.
2. a) What philosophical problems are raised by religious belief in 'life after death'? **b)** Discuss how far such problems are capable of being solved.

Question 1 contains a statement of a view. One of the best ways of answering a question of this type of structure is first to give reasons for agreeing with the statement and then arguing the case against. Remember to make clear how your argument shows that life after death is likely or unlikely. Data needs interpreting and relating back to the argument.

You might like to try to answer question 2 by drawing a spider diagram that shows both the actual problems and also attempts at replying to them. Perhaps you might also like to try responding to the replies.

14 Religious language

1 God talk

KEY ISSUE One of the strongest attacks on the arguments for the existence of God in recent times has come from linguistic philosophy. The assumption in the theistic proofs is that God is an external, independent objective being. This is to regard statements about God as *cognitive*. Cognitive statements are statements that are true or false in the ways that literal statements are true or false. However other philosophers see religious statements as more *non-cognitive* (i.e. not open to truth or falsity at all). In this other sense, coming to see that there is a God involves seeing a new meaning in one's life, and being given a new understanding. There is no new fact to discover, but rather seeing what is already here in a completely new way.

Certainly religious talk poses difficulties. Someone may say that 'God is love'. However, it might not be clear what this actually means. What does 'God' mean? And 'love' is meaningful when used to refer to human activities – but can it be applied to God? Would it mean the same?

Another example that I have used is 'God is timeless' (*Religious Language*, 1994). As I commented:

> the difficulty with this statement is that it is not possible to explain the word 'timeless'. Everything we experience happens in time and it is difficult to understand something that is not in time. The heart of the problem seems to be that religious terms attempt to refer to things beyond anyone's experience. They describe the 'infinite', the 'mysterious' and other metaphysical ideas that are not dealt with by our everyday language and it is thus difficult to see whether religious terms have meaning.

What lies behind these two different approaches, cognitive and non-cognitive, is a different understanding of 'truth'. The cognitive approach assumes a 'correspondence theory of truth' as opposed to a 'coherence theory of truth', and is followed by philosophers known as **realists** since for them what makes a statement true or false is whether it corresponds to the state of affairs which it attempts to depict. As Peter Vardy says:

> ... realists maintain that reality is separate from our language and that our language stretches out to a reality that is external to us and tries to express it accurately.

> *The Puzzle of God* (1990), p. 16

In contrast are the **anti-realists**, who assume a 'coherence theory of truth'. For them a statement is true if it fits in (coheres) with other true statements. Truth is relative to the community who are making the statements. So, in a sense, they *make* religious truths rather than *discover* them.

To understand these varying approaches and how they came about it is necessary to review how religious language has been understood in the past.

Another way of expressing the debate about realism and anti-realism with regards to religious language is to highlight two key issues. One concerns 'universals', i.e. nouns like 'person' and 'goodness'. The issue is whether they are rooted:

- in some reality in things, or
- in something beyond things, or
- in human constructions.

The other key issue concerns how to interpret religious texts: -

● literally
● allegorically
● symbolically.

Traditionally, there have been three main approaches to these issues, and all three were reflected in the medieval period.

a) Equivocal language about God

Equivocal means that the same word is used with a totally different meaning or in a vague or ambiguous way. For instance, the word 'post' can have at least two very different meanings. If language about God is equivocal then it becomes difficult to know what is being stated about God. This approach led to the Via Negativa (negative way). The Via Negativa argues that it is impossible to speak of God by means of positive attributes. Instead one emphasises what God is *not*, drawing attention to His otherness and unknowability. If religious language is equivocal, then by denying all descriptions of God you get insight and experience of God rather than unbelief and scepticism. In this approach language is functional and evocative, rather than cognitive and descriptive.

However, this approach has been criticised on the grounds that theists do seem to want to make positive assertions. The listing of things God is not seems insufficiently limiting to lead to any clear attribute.

b) Univocal language about God

Whilst some figurative language may be in the Bible, it is clear that meaningful revelation has been given. Therefore religious language must be **univocal**, that is, the words used about God must have the same meaning or be as clear as the words that are used about the universe. However, some argue that the implication would then be that God is part of the universe, since the language has the same meaning.

c) Analogical language about God

Analogy is the compromise between the other two positions. God is *not* a being like other beings *but* we can reason about Him. Aquinas argued that all such words about God are non-literal but are analogical. They elucidate the relationship between a term used of one thing and that term when used of another. Analogical language is not an instrument for mapping out the divine attributes but is a means by which we may be compared to God (father / good / loving), in order in some way to describe God's nature, when His existence is already presupposed.

Hence according to Aquinas, language about God is neither equivocal or univocal. For instance, God is not 'good' in exactly the same sense as people may be, nor is He 'good' in a completely unrelated way. It is argued that for the analogy to be valid there must be points of correspondence between language and its object. Colin Brown suggests that God has revealed Himself in action, thought and word. Therefore because of religious experience, such analogical language is appropriate and meaningful. 'Divine truth has to be refracted and expressed in terms of human words and finite images' (*Philosophy and the Christian Faith,*1968, p. 32).

Analogies can be subdivided into two types.

i) Analogy of attribution

This analogy contains the concept of derivation. There is a causal relationship, e.g. human wisdom is a reflection of God's wisdom. Hick goes further and discriminates between 'downwards' and 'upwards' analogy. In the former case he draws on the example of a dog's 'faithfulness' to its master, saying that true faithfulness is known directly in ourselves, whereas the dim and imperfect faithfulness of dogs is known only by analogy. In the 'upwards' analogy (from people to God), it is our directly-known love, wisdom, etc. which are 'the shadows and remote approximations' to the perfect qualities of God. These are known to us only by analogy. Hence, to say that God is loving is meaningful even if it is not clear what exactly it means. It is meaningful because love is a human attribute and there is a causal connection between humans and God. God is the cause of everything so God is love because God is the cause of love.

Since God is infinite, terms that are capable of infinite expression are more applicable than terms that are not. Thus 'God is loving' is more appropriate than 'God is a rock'. The latter example Aquinas calls a 'metaphor'. Surprisingly, in the twentieth century this view has been reversed and the emphasis is now on metaphors (see page 128).

ii) Analogy of proportionality

This analogy states that the attributes of God are in the same way proportional to His nature as the attributes of humans are proportional to their nature. Cabbages have life, Peter Cole has life, God has life. There is a proportionate relationship. In the case of God, the proportion is extended.

One criticism that has been raised about this approach is that proportion is only meaningful when both terms are known. But we neither know God nor the proportionate life. Therefore the analogy is seen as pointless. For a good critique of analogies see Chapter 2 in *The Philosophy of Religious Language* by Dan Stiver (1996).

2 Empiricism and the Vienna Circle

> **KEY ISSUE** Twentieth-century English philosophy has been
> dominated by language analysis.

As has been noted, both metaphysical and theological language faces
the difficulty of speaking intelligibly of that which is ultimate,
transcendent or perfect. The movement in the twentieth century
based around Logical Positivism centred on the univocal approach to
language. Logical positivists decided that such language, when
applied to God, was not just false but meaningless! Logical positivists
were so named because 'they recognised only the positive sciences
(as against systems of metaphysical speculation) as valid sources of
human knowledge, and in this process attended to the logical
structure of scientific (that is, acceptable) statements.' (*Collins
Dictionary of Philosophy*, 1990).

In the 1920s and 1930s, many philosophers dedicated a lot of
discussion to the 'criteria of meaning' issue. (The question may be
put as 'what is the meaning of "meaning"?') They were trying to
develop rules for meaningful discourse. One group of philosophers,
based in Vienna, has become known as the Vienna Circle and
included philosophers such as Schlick (1882–1936) and Carnap
(1891–1970).

Accepting that knowledge is based on experience, they felt that
this could also be applied to language. A criterion of meaning could
be established. The Vienna Circle felt that experience is the key to
determining whether a sentence is meaningful or not. They took the
view that cognitive language expresses an empirical state of affairs.
Determining which words can be judged either 'meaningful' or
'meaningless' is referred to as applying *criteria of meaning.*

a) The Verification Principle

The Logical Positivists formulated the **Verification Principle,** which
they argued was a logical principle about the meaning of words. For
a statement to be meaningful it had to be verifiable by the sense
experiences (sight, touch, taste, smell, hearing). This eliminated
metaphysical statements. It was not an issue about whether the
statements were true or false, but rather that they were without
meaning. A major influence on this group was the work of
Wittgenstein. His book *Tractatus Logico-Philosophicus* (1922) argued
for a picture theory of language. This stressed that language had to
be about something other than language. Meaningful language
involved words being defined by the real world of objects. The
meaning of a proposition lay in knowing what is pictured. To
understand a proposition means to know what is the case if it is true.

Unfortunately his work was misunderstood, since he believed that the mystical was important and could only be spoken about in equivocal language. He even read poetry to the Vienna Circle!

However, this strong form of the Verification Principle excluded various statements that could not be absolutely verified but that many considered meaningful. For example, historical statements such as 'Julius Caesar landed at Deal in 55 BC' or general laws of science such as 'all metals expand when heated.' could not be absolutely verified. After all, it is not possible to observe (and therefore verify) every piece of metal every time it is heated and therefore we cannot state that all metal expands when it is heated.

It was considerations such as these that led many philosophers to shy away from such a strict application of the Verification Principle (although some members of the Vienna Circle, e.g. Schlick, argued that such things as scientific laws were meaningless: they were nonsense but 'useful nonsense'). One philosopher who attempted to reinterpret the Verification Principle was A J Ayer (1910–1989). Although Ayer was not actually a member of the Vienna Circle, his book, *Language, Truth and Logic* (1936), is probably the most famous description of Logical Positivism.

Ayer argued for a weak form of the Verification Principle. He rejected conclusive verifiability and instead argued that, for meaningfulness, it was sufficient just to be able to know what sense experience would make the statement probable. However, even this is not possible for religious statements since 'the notion of a person whose essential attributes are non-empirical is not an intelligible notion at all' (*Language, Truth and Logic,* p. 154). He felt that, through the misuse of language, people assumed that because a word existed there must be some corresponding reality.

b) Criticisms of the Verification Principle

Are, therefore, religious statements to be considered meaningless? The Verification Principle should give no reason to believe this; indeed it is probably one of the most discredited theories of the twentieth century.

The Verification Principle cannot itself be verified. There is no sense experience that could count in its favour: the theory itself is not verifiable. Thus if we accepted the theory, we would have to argue that the theory itself is meaningless. In reply, the Logical Positivists said that the Verification Principle was not a true statement but merely a recommendation for the use of words. However, if that were so, many felt that it was a recommendation that one could ignore! It rejected statements that people felt were meaningful and therefore was not a good definition of 'meaningful'.

● Keith Ward (*Holding Fast to God*, 1982) stated that the Verification Principle excluded nothing, since all experiences are allowable because of the criterion of 'verifiable in principle'. He argues that the existence of God can be verified in principle since 'If I were God I would be able to check the truth of my own existence' (p. 18).

● John Hick felt that the criteria demanded by the Logical Positivists could be met by 'eschatological verification'. He cites the illustration of two men walking down the same road. One believed that this road led to the Celestial City. The other believed that the road went nowhere. Both interpret signs along the route in different ways. However, verification is possible since there either is or is not a Celestial City. Clearly Hick was thinking of theological statements about the second coming and the existence of heaven. The difficulty with this approach is that there can be no disproof, for if there is no Celestial City, no life after death, no God, then there will be no one to know the falsity of the belief.

● Hick wrote about eschatological verification in response to the University Debate that centred around falsification (see page 126). He was showing that there are limitations to the Falsification Principle, since the Celestial City could be verified eschatologically but *not* falsified.

● Theological statements are also acceptable by the Verification Principle since 'Jesus was raised from the dead' is a historical statement, which is therefore acceptable.

● A J Ayer later admitted (*The Central Questions of Philosophy*, 1973) the inadequacy of the criteria for verification in that it allowed all statements to be classed as meaningful. For a fuller discussion on this read Brian Davies, *An Introduction to the Philosophy of Religion* (1993), pp. 5–9.

It should be noted that Logical Positivists made a distinction between a statement that was meaningful and a statement that was true (or false). The criterion of meaning was concerned to distinguish statements that were meaningful. The issue of whether the statements were true or false was a different area of discussion.

c) The Falsification Principle

In the 1950s Anthony Flew looked at the problem from a different perspective. He proposed that a statement was meaningless if no sense experience can ever count against it (i.e. if nothing could ever happen that would change a person's belief in it being true, it could never be shown to be false and therefore was meaningless). This was known as the **Falsification Principle**.

Flew was prompted in this approach by the writings of a philosopher of science, Sir Karl Popper, who suggested it was not 'verifiability' with which science tested hypotheses, but 'falsifiability'. Hence Flew argued that if you knew what observation to make which would show the statement to be false, then the statement would be synthetic and meaningful. Some people regard his Falsification

Principle as a new criterion of meaningfulness, whilst others see it as a variation of the verification criterion.

Flew illustrated this by a parable about the challenge to belief, previously used by John Wisdom. In it he clearly presupposes the falsification criterion. He tells of two explorers who discover a clearing that resembles a humanly-made garden yet in other ways resembles a natural phenomenon. One explorer is convinced that there is a gardener; the other disagrees. They set about to test the hypothesis that there is a gardener, using fences, bloodhounds, etc. No evidence of a gardener turns up. However, at every stage the believer qualifies the hypothesis: the gardener comes at night; he is invisible; he cannot be detected by any of the senses. Finally the non-believer asks: 'Just how does what you call an invisible, intangible, eternally elusive gardener differ from an imaginary gardener or even from no gardener at all?' (from 'Theology and Falsification', in *New Essays in Philosophical Theology*, 1955, pp. 96–99).

Flew's claim is that this is what often happens to religious claims: 'Death by a thousand qualifications.' It is similar to the response in the face of evil that says 'God's ways are mysterious'. For the non-believer there seems no difference between a God that loves, a God that does not love and no God at all!

Flew was showing that a statement can only be regarded as meaningful if some state or event can be specified, such that if it occurred it would falsify the statement. In other words, to assert something is to deny something else. Hence if nothing is ruled out, nothing is being asserted. If a statement is compatible with everything else, then it is not asserting anything. It is not saying anything unique. He felt that religious believers kept qualifying their claims to avoid falsification, which ultimately produced 'death by a thousand qualifications'.

d) Criticisms of the Falsification Principle

Flew seemed to be suggesting that religious assertions had no empirical consequences (since they asserted nothing), hence his view brought forth a number of responses. These were published in the journal *University* and are referred to as the 'University Debate'. Strangely enough, although the debate was about univocal language, they used parables to illustrate their points.

- **Hare and 'bliks'**: Hare thought Flew was right about the problem of falsification and agreed that religious language may be non-cognitive, *but* held that religious statements were still meaningful and important. He regarded religious beliefs as **'bliks'**, which was his term for unfalsifiable convictions but none the less important for the result they have on our conduct. He illustrated this by the parable about the lunatic who thought all dons were trying to murder him (see page 75).

● **Mitchell**: Mitchell agrees that statements about God are assertions but disagrees with Flew and claims that religious statements can be falsified in principle, though not in practice. He illustrates his view with the story of the resistance leader (see page 82). This parable shows that the religious believer displays an attitude of trust and that religious statements are not neutral hypotheses. It is not that things do not count against the faithfulness of the resistance leader; rather they may not decisively overturn the evidence in favour. Relating this to religious belief – evil counts against God's love – the trust is not without a sense of tension and conflict. However, if the believer has good reason to trust God's love, then evil may not be sufficient reason to overthrow that trust. Thus you can empirically falsify it, but it is difficult to say how much contrary evidence it requires to reach that point.

Both Hare and Mitchell were accepting that falsification to some extent could be used as a criterion for determining meaningfulness. However, there do seem to be problems with the Falsification Principle:

● **Richard Swinburne** (*The Coherence of Theism*, 1977) claimed that statements can have meaning yet they cannot be falsified. He uses the illustration of toys that come to life at night only when they cannot be detected. There is no means by which the claim about toys can be falsified. However, the statement conveys meaning and hence goes against the claims of the Falsification Principle. Likewise John Hick used the story of the Celestial City (see page 125) to show that some things could only be verified and not falsified, yet were still meaningful.
● Like the Verification Principle, the Falsification Principle fails its own test. For the Principle to count as a meaningful assertion there must be things that would count against its truth. However, it is not clear what would count as evidence against it!

3 Symbolic language

It is now generally agreed that the ideas of 'verification' and 'falsification' are rather narrow and do not provide a criterion for establishing meaning. Many philosophers and theologians have used the idea when discussing religious language that something can represent something else. In other words they think that it is possible to say something meaningful about God even though what they are saying may not be literal.

a) Symbols

This approach sees religious language as symbolic. The term **symbol** often has with it the implication of superficiality, but this is to misunderstand. A symbol is something that has deep communicative power and evokes participation in the intended meaning (as opposed to 'sign' which impacts on the intellect only).

Perhaps the best known and most radical supporter of the view that religious language is symbolic, was Paul Tillich (1885–1965). He argued that 'God talk' is symbolic and cannot therefore be translated into literal assertions.

> Symbolic language alone is able to express the ultimate because it transcends the capacity of any finite reality to express it directly.
>
> (*Dynamics of Faith*, 1958).

Tillich preferred to speak of 'Being' rather than the words and deeds of a God who exists over and above the world and breaks into it. In his book *Systematic Theology*, (1951) God is defined as 'that which concerns us ultimately', or 'the ground of our being'. Hence God is not a Being (who may or may not exist) but Being itself. In fact it is just as much atheistic to say God exists as to deny it. God can be described as personal but He is not a person; if He was He would be finite. It is only the person, who in complete seriousness can say that life is shallow, who is an atheist.

This approach to the doctrine of God is still quite popular, John Robinson, then Bishop of Woolwich, in his book *Honest to God* (1963) was the most influential populariser of his views. More recently, Don Cupitt (*Taking Leave of God*, 1980) has written an attack on the traditional Christian doctrine of God and uses concepts similar to those of Tillich.

This approach by Don Cupitt argues that religious language should no longer be seen as being about the transcendent or the metaphysical as really it is about things that we all experience. The problems of religious language therefore disappear, as religious language is no longer seen to be about things that are beyond experience. Indeed what religion is all about, according to some, is not some external being but our own psychology and feelings. This approach has become known as *reductionism*. For D Z Phillips (*Death and Immortality*, 1971) the phrase 'eternal life' has nothing to do with living forever; rather, it is concerned with our own psychology and the quality of life that we should be experiencing now.

Needless to say, such views have brought strong reactions. For instance, Keith Ward wrote the book *Holding Fast to God* (1982) as a direct reply to Don Cupitt's *Taking Leave of God*.

b) Metaphors

Likewise a **metaphor** creates participation whereby its truth is experienced. Interestingly, the role of metaphor has taken central stage in the late twentieth century. Mark Johnson (*Philosophical Perspectives on Metaphors*, 1981) said, 'We are in the midst of a metaphormania.' Two recent contributors to this debate are Janet Soskice and Sallie McFague.

In particular, Soskice (*Metaphor and Religious Language*, 1985) defends the realist claim that such language reveals something about God rather than referring to the believer's attitude or stance towards God or life. Her argument involves comparing metaphors and models in religion to their use in science (e.g. 'the brain is a computer').

McFague (*Models of God in Religious Language*, 1982) sees not only religious language but theology itself as metaphorical (i.e. theology is organised by root metaphors). She also favours new metaphors since the old ones of Father, Son and Kingdom are patriarchal. She suggests that the Trinity can be seen as 'mother, lover and friend'.

It is difficult to decide whether a symbol can successfully represent that which is beyond our experience. There seems to be no way to judge whether a symbol is adequate. Neither is there any way to determine whether a symbol gives the wrong insights about the ultimate (i.e. is it appropriate?).

c) Myths

The **myth** is the most complex type of symbolic language since it incorporates symbols, metaphors and models. To many people, to speak of myths is to say that something is untrue. However, a modern understanding sees myths as giving insights into human existence. The problem has been that we have applied our scientific ideas to the myths and judged the originators as naive and simple. Instead we needed to decipher them and understand that the language is symbolic. They are often associated with rites-of-passage events and so seek to provide a framework within which the whole of life can be understood. Time and space are seen as symbolic, so that those myths about origins are to be interpreted as being about all the happenings that take place in a person's time. These myths should also be seen in the context of coming from communities that held a religious outlook on the world and so interpreted life accordingly.

Probably the best-known scholar dealing with myths is Bultmann. He gave the New Testament an existentialist interpretation and many felt that he reduced it to a secular philosophy. The view that the New Testament contains many myths has most recently been expressed by David Jenkins, former Bishop of Durham.

d) Models

A twentieth-century development of the traditional idea of analogy can be seen in the work of Ian Ramsey (*Religious Language*, 1957). He saw religious language functioning as stories or models, qualified in various ways such that they bring about a disclosure which in turn leads to a religious kind of response – a commitment of a total kind. A model is a representation of something which assists us to understand the original. In terms of religious language a model is a 'situation with which we are all familiar, and which can be used for reaching another situation with which we are not so familiar' (p. 61). Models are usually accompanied by 'qualifiers'. These point to the way in which the model is to be developed. For instance, consider the phrase 'infinitely good'. 'Good' is the model and 'infinite' is the qualifier. The model begins a series in our understanding of 'good'. The qualifier 'infinite' is a directive stimulating us to go on … and on … and on … until it dawns on us that when we talk of God we are not talking of something which is comparatively superior. Rather it is that which evokes adoration, wonder, worship, commitment (p. 68).

In this way, Ramsey argues that the use of the word 'infinite' does not result in the language ending in an 'empirical void'. Theological phrases are not seen as labels to objective facts but the means to evoke a disclosure of that which lies beyond what is immediately observed.

e) Language-games

These ideas about language being functional and 'creating participation' rather than 'illustrating information', are based, in part, on the work of the philosopher Ludwig Wittgenstein (1889-1951). Early on in his philosophical career Wittgenstein put forward a 'picture theory of meaning'. On this view the primary function of words is to name objects and the meaning of a word is the object it stands for. Hence being wrong about meaning is being wrong about the correlates between words and things.

However, later on he re-examined the question of meaning and came to a different conclusion. He argued that it is unrealistic to suppose that all words are ultimately based on pictures and pointed out that language is used in a variety of different ways. His ideas can be found in his *Philosophical Investigations* (published in 1953, two years after his death).

Wittgenstein centred on the way that language works and the uses to which it is put. He saw that the problems of religious language were caused by the misunderstanding of language. He was not so concerned with the truth and falsity of language but with the way it was used and the functions it performed. He coined the phrase 'Don't ask for the meaning, ask for the use'.

Wittgenstein likened language to a game that we play. This is because at the heart of Wittgenstein's concept of '**language-games**' is the idea that words only have meaning because of their context and therefore we have to be careful to know which 'game' we are playing. For example, the word 'castling' (a move in chess) has no meaning if we are playing netball. Wittgenstein then applied this idea to philosophy and concluded that philosophical problems about language are created by not understanding that words can be used in different language-games. Hence his statement that 'philosophical problems arise when language goes on holiday'. Wittgenstein gave the example of the problems associated with the word 'soul' and argued that these problems are caused by trying to see the soul as some sort of physical object. The problems, according to Wittgenstein, would be dissolved if it was realised that the 'physical object' game simply does not apply to the soul.

The term 'language-game' is meant to highlight the fact that the speaking of a language is part of an activity. Meaning emerges in the context of human activity *not* from dependence on correspondence between word and object. Wittgenstein argued that we do not so much discover the rules of how to use a word but rather we agree upon it. Hence meaning is convention! A meaning mistake is about not applying the word in the right way. The public, shared language-game is what counts as the right way. These rules Wittgenstein called 'grammar'. To say that God has big feet is not to play according to the rules because convention says that this is inappropriate to God.

The phrase / concept of 'language-games' is seen as particularly appropriate. In an article on 'Language games' in *Dialogue* Issue 7, Felicity McCutcheon drew some parallels between games and language:

- There is no unique object that can be said to be the meaning of the word 'game'. Likewise there is no one meaning of a particular word.
- There are many different games (e.g. chess, netball, etc) each of which has its own rules. Learning to play means learning the rules. Likewise with language it involves learning what you can and cannot say.
- Games involve participation. Likewise the speaking of a language is part of an activity. Participation involves being understood (i.e. playing to the rules).
- Games are not reality. Likewise meaningfulness of discourse is determined by language users and not by reality.
- Making a wrong move is equivalent to applying words in the wrong way.
- You can't do that = You can't say that.

This understanding of religious language has led to the view that each language-game is immune from charges of incoherence and irrationality, since it has its own internal criteria of coherence and intelligibility. The danger of such a view is that each area of life develops its own unique criteria of meaning and truth. For example, Felicity McCutcheon (*Dialogue* Issue 7) uses the illustration of the question 'Was Jesus God?' According to Neo-Wittgensteinians it cannot be given a yes / no answer; rather it depends on which game you are in when you ask the question. (A Jew and a Christian might give different but equally valid answers.)

In addition the Neo-Wittgensteinian account of religious language has made the controversial claim that it cannot be understood as reality-depicting. It should be noted that Wittgenstein never made this judgement, only his followers (e.g. D Z Philips). However, many feel that religious statements do entail a truth that is not entirely dependent on the context. Indeed, many religious claims are claims that are believed to be true for everyone, for example, the claim in Christianity that Jesus died in order to bring salvation.

f) Conclusions

Not surprisingly, there has yet to appear a theory of religious language that has won general acceptance. Given that religious faith seeks to provide an understanding of reality that incorporates all the component parts of our experiences, it is to be expected that religious language turns out to be complex. Linguistic analysis has served the purpose of drawing attention to this fact, but has often fallen into the error of reductionism, as well as denying any cognitive sense. Instead, perhaps it should make us aware that many of the theories may reveal different insights into the structure of a complex whole.

Answering questions on Chapter 14

Some questions tend to require a general overview of the issues, so that students can select the illustrations, especially to illustrate the non-cognitive. Examples of typical questions are:

1. 'All talk about God is both without meaning and without purpose'. Discuss.
2. **a)** What is meant by 'language-games'? **b)** Why have some scholars claimed that religious language is a language-game? **c)** Evaluate other scholars' arguments for rejecting this claim.
3. **a)** In what ways has the meaningfulness of religious language been challenged by twentieth-century empiricism? **b)** How have such challenges been met and with what degree of success?
4. 'Once we acknowledge the symbolic character of religious language, can we be sure we are talking about anything at all?' Discuss.

Question 1 demands discussion on both meaning and purpose. Views that reject talk of God as meaningful will include logical positivists approach. Remember to evaluate this approach and its basic assumptions. Purpose of non-cognitive religious language should include evocativeness, giving insight, and expressing trust/commitment/ worship. Question 3 needs to include 'The University' debate but avoiding just paraphrasing the parables without any context or discussion as to how they contribute to an explanation. Often examiners read the story retold by the candidate and are left asking 'so what?' when the point of the story is not explained.

Bibliography

W Alston, *Divine Nature and Human Language* (Cornell University Press, 1989).

Augustine, *Confessions* (Penguin, 1961).

Augustine, *The City of God* (Penguin, 1972, new edition 1984).

A J Ayer, *The Central Questions of Philosophy* (Penguin, 1976).

A J Ayer, *Language, Truth and Logic* (Penguin, 1971).

P Badham, *Immortality or Extinction?* (Macmillan, 1982).

C Brown, *Philosophy and the Christian Faith* (IVP, 1968).

M Buber, *I and Thou* (T&T Clark, 1937).

S Clark, *How To Live Forever* (Routledge, 1995).

A C Clarke, *World of Strange Powers* (Guild, 1985).

W Clifford, *Lectures and Essays* (London, 1879).

P Cole & J Lee, *Religious Language* (Abacus, 1994).

D Cupitt, *Taking Leave of God* (SCM, 1980).

M Curd, *Argument and Analysis: An Introduction to Philosophy* (West Publishing Company, 1992).

A Custance, *The Mysterious Matter of Mind* (Grand Rapids, 1980).

B Davies, *An Introduction to the Philosophy of Religion* (OUP, 1993).

B Davies (ed.), *Philosophy of Religion: A Guide to the Subject* (Cassell, 1998).

B Davies, *Thinking about God* (Chapman, 1985).

C Davies, *The Evidential Force of Religious Experience* (Oxford, 1989).

S Davis, *Encountering Evil* (John Knox, 1981).

S Davis, *God, Reason and Theistic Proofs* (Edinburgh University Press, 1997).

S N Deane, (ed), *St Anselm: Basic Writings* (LaSalle, 1962).

R Descartes, *A Discourse on Method* (Everyman,1995 reprint).

F Dostoyevsky, *The Brothers Karamazov* (Penguin, 1958 reprint).

C S Evans, *Thinking about Faith* (IVP, 1985).

A Flew & A MacIntyre, (ed.) *New Essays in Philosophical Theology* (SCM, 1955).

J Glover, *The Philosophy and Psychology of Personal Identity* (Penguin, 1988).

C Hartshorne, *The Logic of Perfection* (La Salle, 1962).

D Hay, *Inner Space* (Oxford, 1987).

J Hick, *The Existence of God* (Macmillan, 1964).

J Hick, *Evil and the God of Love* (Fontana, 1968).

J Hick, *Arguments for the Existence of God* (Macmillan, 1970).

J Hick, *Death and Eternal Life* (Collins, 1976).

J Hick, *Philosophy of Religion* (Prentice-Hall, 1983).

R Holland, *The Miraculous* (American Philosophical Quarterly 2, 1965).

J Hosper, *An Introduction to Philosophical Analysis* (4th edition) (Routledge, 1997).

D Hume, *Dialogues concerning Natural Religion* (Bobbs-Merrill Educational Publishing, 1970 reprint).

D Hume, *Enquiries concerning Human Understanding* (First published 1777).

W James, *The Varieties of Religious Experience* (Penguin, 1902 reprint 1983).

M Johnson, *Philosophical Perspectives on Metaphors* (University of Minnesota Press, 1981).

I Kant, *The Critique of Pure Reason* Trans by N Kemp Smith (St Martins, 1965).

C S Lewis, *A Grief Observed* (Faber, 1961).

C S Lewis, *The Problem of Pain* (London, Centenary Press, 1940).

D MacKay, *The Clockwork Image* (IVP, 1974).

J Mackie, *The Miracle of Theism* (Oxford, 1982).

B Magee, *The Story of Philosophy* (Dorling Kindersley, 1998).

F Ma'sumiansee, *Life after Death* (One World, 1995).

S McFague, *Models of God in Religious Language* (Fortress, 1982).

A McGrath, *Christian Theology: An Introduction* (Blackwell, 1994).

A McKinnon, *Miracles and Paradox* (American Philosophical Quaterly 4, 1967).

R Messer, *Does God's Existence need Proof?* (Clarendon, 1997).

J S Mill, *Three Essays on Religion* (Longmans Green, 1874).

H Montefiore, *The Probability of God* (SCM, 1985).

R Moody, *Life after Life* (Bantam, 1975).

J Newman, *Grammar of Assent* (Notre Dame/London 1979).

M Oliver, *Hamlyn History: Philosophy* (Hamlyn, 1997).

R Otto, *The Idea of the Holy* (OUP, 1923).

W Paley, *Natural Theology* (Ibis, 1986).

T Penelhum, *Survival and Disembodied Existence* (Routledge, 1970).

W Penfield, *The Physical Basis of Mind* (Blackwell, 1950).

A Plantinga, *The Nature of Necessity* (Oxford, 1974).

D Z Phillips, *Death and Immortality* (Macmillan, 1971).

A Plantinga, *God, Freedom and Evil* (Eerdmans, 1974).

K Popper & J Eccles, *The Self and Its Brain* (London, 1977).

H Price, *Survival and the Idea of 'Another World'* (Proceedings of the Society for Psychical Research 50, Part 182, Jan 1953).

J Puddefoot, *God and the Mind Machine* (SPCK, 1996).

I Ramsey, *Religious Language* (SCM, 1957).

J Rhine, *Extrasensory Perception* (Society for Psychical Research, 1935).

J Robinson, *Honest to God* (SCM, 1963).

B Russell, *Why I am not a Christian* (Unwins, 1957).

G Ryle, *The Concept of Mind* (Penguin, 1949).

N Smart, *Philosophers and Religious Truth* (SCM, 1964).

R Solomon, *The Big Questions* (Harcourt Brace, 1998).

J Soskice, *Metaphor and Religious Language* (Clarendon, 1985).

W Stace, *Mysticism and Philosophy* (Macmillan, 1960).

R Stannard, *The God Experiment* (Faber, 1999).

D Stiver, *The Philosophy of Religious Language* (Blackwell, 1996).

St Teresa, *The Collected Works of St. Teresa of Avila* (ICS Publications, 1987).

R Swinburne, *The Coherence of Theism* (Clarendon, 1977).

R Swinburne, *The Concept of Miracle* (Macmillan, 1970).

R Swinburne, *The Existence of God* (OUP, 1979).

R Swinburne, *Is There a God?* (OUP, 1996).

F R Tennant, *Philosophical Theology* (CUP, 1930).

A Thiselton, *A Concise Encyclopedia of the Philosophy of Religion* (One World, 2002).

M Thompson, *Teach Yourself Philosophy of Religion* (Hodder & Stoughton, 1997)

P Tillich, *Systematic Theology* (Nisbet & Co, 1951).

P Tillich, *Dynamics of Faith* (Harper & Bros, 1958).

P Vardy, *The Puzzle of God* (Collins, 1990).

G Vesey, P Foulkes, *Collins Dictionary of Philosophy* (Collins, 1990).

W Wainwright, *Philosophy of Religion* (Wadsworth, 1988).

K Ward, *Holding Fast to God* (One World, 1982).

J Webber, *Revelation and Religious Experience* (Abacus, 1995).

E Wiesel, *The Trial of God* (Penguin, 1979).

M Wiles, *God's Action in the World* (SCM, 1986).

I Wilson, *The After Death Experience* (Guild, 1987).

L Wittgenstein, *Tractatus Logico-Philosophicus* (Routledge, 1961(1921)).

L Wittgenstein, *Philosophical Investigations* (Blackwell, 1953).

R Zaehner, *Concordant Discord* (Oxford, 1970).

C Zaleski, *Otherworld Journeys* (OUP, 1988).

Further Reading

General coverage
D Palmer, *Does the Centre Hold?* (Mayfield, 1996).
M Peterson, *Reason and Religious Belief* (OUP, 1991).
M Peterson, *Philosophy of Religion, Selected Readings* (OUP, 1996).
B Magee, *The Story of Philosophy* (Dorling Kindersley, 1998).
M Oliver, *Hamlyn History: Philosophy* (Hamlyn, 1997).
M Thompson, *Teach Yourself Philosophy of Religion* (Hodder, 1997).

Arguments (Chapter 1)
N Warburton, *Thinking from A–Z* (Routledge, 1996).

Nature of God (Chapter 2)
R Nash, *The Concept of God* (Grand Rapids, 1983).
H P Owen, *Concepts of Deity* (Macmillan, 1971).
K Rogers, *Perfect Being Theology* (Edinburgh University Press, 2000).

Existence of God arguments (Chapters 3–7)
M Palmer, *The Question of God* (Routledge, 2001).
S Davis, *God, Reason and Theistic Proofs* (Edinburgh University Press, 1997).

Miracles (Chapters 8)
C Bloomberg, *The Historical Reliability of the Gospels* (IVP, 1987).
N Cantwell, *Miracles* (Abacus, 2001).
R Geivett (ed.), *In Defence of Miracles* (Apollos, 1997).

The value of theistic proofs (Chapters 9)
R Messer, *Does God's Existence Need Proof?* (Clarendon, 1997).

Faith and reason (Chapters 10)
J Webber, *Faith and Reason* (Abacus, 1995).

Problem of evil (Chapter 11)
S Davis, *Encountering Evil* (John Knox, 1981).
J Hick, *Evil and the God of Love* (Macmillan reprint, 1991).

Mind and body (Chapter 12)
P Carruthers, *Introducing Persons* (Routledge, 1994).

Life after death (Chapter 13)
F Ma'sumian, *Life after Death* (One World, 1995).

Religious language (Chapter 14)
B Magee, *Confessions of a Philosopher* (Phoenix, 1998).
D Stiver, *The Philosophy of Religious Language* (Blackwell, 1996).

Index